RETURN
—— OF A ——
REFUGEE

The Compelling Story of Eric Willise Wowoh

Written by
Eric Willise Wowoh

Return Of A Refuge
by Eric Willise Wowoh

Printed in the United States of America.

ISBN 9781498485517

Website: www.returnofarefugee.com

Email Address is: info@returnofarefugee.com

www.xulonpress.com

Dedication

This book is dedicated to God Almighty and to all of those who lost their childhood through war, natural disaster, poverty and abandonment;

In gratitude to all those who help to bring hope and opportunity to a hurting world.

"Truly I tell you, whatever you did for one of the least
of these brothers and sisters of mine, you did for me."
Matthew 25:40

Table of Contents

Introduction

When I was two years old, my parents relocated our family to Bong Mines in Lower Bong County, Central Liberia, Africa. We lived in a village near Bong Mines until the brutal Liberian Revolution started in 1989 and separated our entire family for about twenty years, and the lives of many were destroyed.

During the war I was captured as a child by rebels, beaten, tortured and left to die. Miraculously I escaped and spent fourteen years living in eleven different refugee camps. When I was twenty-three and living in a refugee camp, a friend gave me a computer. I learned how to use the computer and began training other refugees from all over Africa. My team and I established Change Agent Network, and we have impacted the lives of many across the world through the origins of that one single desktop computer. In 2006 the U.S. government, in collaboration with the Migration and Refugees Services of the Conference of Catholic Bishops of America, brought me to America in a refugee resettlement program.

This book, *Return of a Refugee*, contains the details of my life story. I never thought about writing it for publication until two Lafayette writers, Carol Stubbs and Nancy Rust, approached me about writing a children's book based on my story. They convinced me that my story needed to be documented. I spent many hours with them talking through my story. It forced me to think about how all the events in my life have led me to where I am now. I could see God's presence in my life through both the painful and good times. From the time I was taken from my home as a refugee minor at age twelve, I had always wanted to return home from exile to reunite with my parents and live in my own country in peace and harmony. After almost two decades I am very grateful I'm finally able to return home and help rebuild my destroyed nation of Liberia and bring hope and opportunity to an impoverished, lost and forgotten generation. I am returning home not as a big man, boss, chief or king over the people, but as a former refugee. I am humbled just to serve the people!

Like me, many of my fellow Liberians left the country to live in exile during the war in Liberia. Some settled in third world and developing nations, and others in developed and advanced nations. Most of us tend to stay away from our former home and our country forever after going through these tragic war experiences. We get out, say a prayer and never return to help those we left behind. We forget our own stories and our roots. We often ignore our opportunities to change the story and create a new culture for the next generation. But, we always belong to the land where we come from, thus: *Return of a Refugee*.

I have experienced the extremes this world has to offer. I've lived in Liberia, one of the poorest countries in the world, and I currently live in the United States, the richest country in the history of mankind, a nation founded on godly principles that has gone on to become the most powerful and influential nation on the face of the earth.

I've seen and experienced brokenness and poverty in both places. Many kinds of poverty exist: physical, mental, relational and spiritual. With physical poverty may come sickness, corruption, hunger and disease.

Mental poverty deprives people of access to a quality education and the knowledge to make informed decisions for themselves and for their children. In relational and spiritual poverty, people are lonely, sad, depressed, dissatisfied, angry and bitter. Often they don't know why.

Before we can overcome any of these types of poverty, we must recognize the problems we all face as human beings. Every form of poverty is extremely dangerous in its own way. Every form has the potential to explode into full-scale violence and destroy lives and properties. Desperate people do desperate things. If we refuse to address these looming problems, we risk repeating history and paying a painful price, often through war and destruction.

Our choices and decisions should be about the children. It is vital that we make the protection and nourishment of the next generation our number-one priority. We must love, teach, discipline and mentor them in the ways of God. We must educate them and provide for them; we must show them the moral responsibility they have to make the world a better place for those who will come after them. We, as parents and leaders, must never forget that those who follow us and who will one day carry the baton of leadership determine the true success and significance of our lives, as well as our legacy. Let the children grow into wisdom and strength. We must make decisions with their future in mind.

When I was born in the early 1970s in Liberia, decisions were often made without serious consideration of the future and what those decisions meant for children and the country. When war broke out, our educational system and our government were destroyed. No one grasped the repercussions of a war that would force many children to become soldiers and would last for more than ten years. Children paid the price for the prior generation's bad decisions—decisions made out of illiteracy, greed, anger and ignorance. Children suffered in the war and in refugee camps because people didn't care enough about them. The war was never about the children; it was all about power, control, money and self.

For those of us who came from these humble backgrounds, who lost our childhood peace and happiness during the war and who are now living in America or other developed nations of the world, it is tempting to think of this as our time of total recovery and entitlement. We reason that we deserve it because of all the pain and suffering we endured. We can easily rationalize the belief that we are at a point in life where we should do nothing but enjoy ourselves and reap some of the benefits and material prosperity this world has to offer. I agree that our early years lacked many of the joys that should be part of a normal childhood. But now is the time for us to step up and give to the children of today a hope we never had. It was not about us when we were children, and it's not about us now. If we sit back and fall into the trap of committing the same sins as those who ruined our childhood, we risk repeating the past.

As one who has spent years growing up as a proud son of Liberia, as well as years wandering through various refugee camps in other African countries, I believe I have a unique insight into the problems that exist in Africa today.

A common refrain is that the problem in Africa is poverty. At face value this belief seems to have some validity. But upon closer examination the poverty argument runs into a serious problem when one considers the continent's tremendous natural resources. It is a well-known fact that Africa has some of the world's largest quantities of diamonds, salt, gold, iron, cobalt, uranium, copper, bauxite, silver and petroleum. In addition, Africa has a large supply of cocoa beans, timber and tropical fruits. Yet many of these resources remain undeveloped.

The disparity between this huge stockpile of available wealth and the extreme poverty can be bridged by a simple solution, education. Africa, specifically Liberia, will never solve its problems unless it deals with the education issue. Government and private aid often fail to address this issue. Most aid focuses on providing basic survival needs such as food, medicine and clothing.

While a need for these things certainly exists, focusing exclusively on them creates a culture of dependence. An old saying is, "Give a man a fish, and you feed him for a day. Teach him how to fish, and you feed him for a lifetime." Many Christian and other nonprofits or nongovernmental organizations focus on providing for the material needs of the African people while neglecting their educational, relational and spiritual needs. Occasionally, some groups focus on evangelism and leave other needs unmet.

A healthy balance is necessary. The people of Africa and Liberia need to hear the gospel and to have their needs met. But, until we can sufficiently educate the people to take care of and provide for themselves, the story will never change.

Part One

My Life Story

1

Born In Fissibu Town

Lofa County, Liberia

I am a native Liberian, born in Fissibu Town, Lofa County, in Northern Liberia. I am the oldest of nine children in my family. Children were named according to the circumstances of their birth. My name, Willise, means illumination and head of family. In our tradition a name has special meaning for the child and sometimes for society.

We had a very primitive lifestyle. I was born at home, and like many native Africans I have no birth certificate or documentation for my birth. We never thought about birthdays or imagined celebrating one. My parents had no education, and they followed the traditional religion of Africa, which was a mixture of Voodoo, Juju and other beliefs. We calculated time by observing the phases of the moon and the seasons.

Fissibu is in a rural part of northern Liberia in Lofa County, one of the fifteen counties in Liberia. Lofa is the second largest county and about one-half the size of the state of New Jersey. It has six local tribes, each with its own language and leadership. My tribe is the Lorma tribe. The different tribes speak many dialects, but the common business or official language is English. Liberian English is different from American or international English.

About fifty families lived in the village. Each of them had a leader, traditionally the oldest male who made all major decisions for the family. A local chief was head of the village—like a mayor. The chief was appointed by elders or heads of the families. A spiritual leader was also appointed and chosen according to his spiritual power. He was as powerful as the leader of the village because people believed he communicated with the gods. Each family had a portion of the village to live in, and living quarters were very close together.

When you ask Africans about family, they think of something beyond the immediate or nuclear family. To them, family includes the extended family: aunts, uncles, grandparents and cousins. About one hundred people were in our family. The family name is considered greater than any individual and always to be protected. The family name always comes first to show its importance.

My parents did not send my siblings and me to school. Many schools were Christian institutions, and most parents did not want children going to Christian schools because they were afraid of what the school would teach. They wanted children to learn the African traditions and acquire native education from their parents and leaders in the village. They also wanted children to help with the daily work of getting food and water for the family.

Before a rural Liberian child could go to school, the whole family had to agree because it meant having one less person available to help at home and on the farm land. It was a big decision to send children to school because their help was necessary. Since we didn't write down birthdates, the test for knowing when children were old enough to go to school was for them to stretch their right arm over their head to the left and then bend it to touch the opposite ear on the left. When their hand covered the ear, they were old enough for school.

When my father was young, they had something called compulsory education. The government hired educational officers to go to villages and towns and force children against their parent's will to go to school. These officers didn't walk through the village like everyone else; they were carried on sedan chairs or on a litter like royalty. They wore fancy clothes and refused to interact with the village people. Parents told children to hide whenever the education officers were in their village. Everyone thought the government was corrupt, and they didn't want government officials educating their children.

Families usually ate one meal a day. We had no meal schedule, no specific eating time. We ate when we were hungry and if food was available. Sometimes we wouldn't eat until eight or nine at night. By the time the meal was ready children might have already fallen asleep and would have to be awakened to eat.

Our house was made of dirt bricks with a metal roof and no indoor plumbing. Children wore a single pair of pants for a year or more, washing them in the river and laying them on a rock to dry. On rare occasions we had shoes to wear.

Although we were very poor, with no hope and opportunity, we had peace with the whole family living together. These were the best days of our lives as children growing up in Liberia. This is the way we lived until the time of the Liberian revolution in 1989.

2

Growing Up In Bong Mines

Bong County, Liberia

My family migrated to Lower Bong County, which borders Lofa County in northern Liberia, when I was about two years old. Most of my childhood memories are from there. My parents moved to Bong Mines because the economy was better near the iron ore mines. The mines were primarily owned by the Bong Mining Company of Germany. The company had built a fenced enclave with electricity, supermarkets, banks, paved roads and even streetlights. Housing was provided for many employees living inside the fenced area. Many settlements sprang up outside the mining enclave. The company people inside the fence depended on Liberians living outside to supply many of their needs, so the economy was fairly good for those outside the fence, which is where we lived. The mining company attracted people from all over the region.

Our life in Bong was fairly primitive. Our daily water came from a hole we dug as a well or from a pump located just outside the fenced area. It was about a thirty-minute walk to the water well or pump, and we carried the water back to our house in buckets on our heads. The children had to carry water every day to provide for the family. Before we could leave the house in the morning, we had to make sure there was enough water for the day.

We fished, hunted and grew our own vegetables for food. The plot of land we farmed was a three-hour walk from the village. We spent six hours just getting to and from our land. The other daylight hours were spent tending the fields. We did all our work manually. We had to carry tools and food to the farm on our heads. Tools were handmade implements: shovels, machetes and axes. We cleared the land, cutting trees and bushes with machetes and axes, and then burned the fields to get rid of the brush. When an animal was caught in the fire, we used it for food. We grew just enough cassava, rice, sweet potatoes, okra, greens and eggplant for our family.

We hunted using bows and arrows as well as sticks sharpened into spears. We mostly hunted birds and small animals like squirrels, bats, groundhogs and rats. We often set traps to catch them. We searched for holes in the ground to find where the animals were hiding. Then we plugged up the holes with fire to drive them out of another entrance. There was no telling what would come out of the holes: snakes, squirrels—all kinds of things.

Sometimes the men set a trap for elephants by digging a very large hole and covering it with brush. When an elephant fell into the hole it was killed for food. That provided enough meat to feed people from several villages, so killing an elephant was cause for a big celebration and feast. The elephant trap also provided the village some protection from rogue elephants.

Occasionally we bought meat, but it was a two-day walk to a village that sold it. We only bought meat when we had something to trade for it: salt, clothing or oil. We also usually brought gifts to exchange.

We fished but had to walk about four hours to find a river with clean water. Runoff from the mines had contaminated the water source near our village. At that time, no conservation laws were in place.

Sometimes I was sent to the marketplace to sell any extra vegetables we had grown. I carried them on my head. It was quite a process to keep them fresh to sell in the market. When greens were harvested, they were carried from the field and spread out on the roof overnight so the dew would fall on them and they wouldn't wilt. Before the sun came up, while everything was still fresh, I put the vegetables in a box and carried them to market on my head. Some days I would make five cents; other days I might make one dollar—that was a good day. I remember my mother using stones like a calculator to help determine how much money she had after selling vegetables.

3

Living In Harbel

Firestone Company Area

One day when I was about eight years old I was on my way to sell vegetables in the market when I met a Liberian deacon by the name of Thomas Tubman. He was from the First Baptist Church near our house in the Bassa Community area in Bong Mines. He stopped me and asked who I was and where I was going and why I wasn't in school. He had a big heart for people, especially children, and he knew my father to be an African religion fundamentalist with strong opinions. The deacon had compassion and wanted to help me go to school. He asked me to come with him to meet his family at his home inside the company area. His wife made bread and needed me to help her sell it. She made bread like shortbread, cornbread and meat pies. In return for my selling the bread, they would feed me and send money to the school so I could attend. My portion of the profits from the sales would go directly to the school for my education.

The next week I started selling bread. I sold it in the morning from about six until eleven and then went to school in the afternoon from one to six. I had to sell about a hundred pieces of bread every morning before school. I carried the bread on my head and sold it outside the fence in the community area. I walked three miles to pick up the bread, sell it, report back and eat at the pastor's house. After that, I walked three miles to school.

Nancy Doe Elementary School was located outside the fenced area. It was made of mud bricks and had a thatched roof. We sat on wooden benches. Each of the six open classrooms held about thirty-five to forty students.

I was one of the oldest students in my class. I had no time to study because of my work and the long walk to get places. I couldn't read in the evening because we had no electricity.

Going to school was a wonderful opportunity for me, but I had to break with my parents over it, and it put a strain on our relationship. They didn't want me to go. They wanted me to stay at home and help. My father was very angry and told me to leave the house. He told my mother not to feed me. Sometimes she hid food in a water bucket, then gave it to me and told me to go get water for the family. This way I could take the food outside and eat without my father knowing. I had no place to stay. Sometimes I slept outside, while at other times I crawled through the window of a friend's room where I would sleep without his parents knowing. I went to this school for two to three years.

My grandfather, my father's father, lived about three hours from my family in Harbel Firestone Rubber Company Headquarters. He was a night security guard at the Firestone Rubber Plantation. He was an African traditionalist and worked during the day doing tribal work. One day he came to visit us at Bong Mines. He wanted me, as the oldest male child, to follow African traditions. He was worried because I had no interest in following in that direction. He said I could live with him at Harbel

Firestone and go to school for free because he was an employee with the company. I moved from Bong Mines to Firestone. Harbel Firestone is located in Margibi County on the north central coast of Liberia. People from all walks of life lived in this place. I then went to the Firestone company school. It was a better school and closer, about thirty minutes away. My grandfather had electricity. I not only had more time to study, I could also study at night. Our life was still poor, but back then it was the best of the best.

My grandfather was a very nice man. People came to him for help with all kinds of problems or illnesses. He used traditional ways of healing. Sometimes he used a live chicken in a ritual sacrifice, or he chanted oracles. At other times he used plants from the forest to help cure sickness. I remember going with him to the cemetery where he talked to the dead. He also saw visions. Often I walked with my grandfather through the forest, and during this time he talked about traditions and healing plants. I picked leaves, and he told me how they helped with a certain illness. He taught me what it meant to be the leader of the family and the oldest male.

4

My Life In War-Time Liberia

After the civil war started in late December 1989, everything became extremely chaotic. My school closed, and my grandfather thought I would be safer living with my parents in Bong Mines. Communication was poor, and nobody knew what was happening in Monrovia, the capital city of Liberia. Some people said the war meant we would have a better life and more freedom. It sounded good at the time, and a lot of people supported this. They knew the government was corrupt and needed to be changed. It took about a year for the war to spread through the entire country. By the time it got to our village, all forms of government had completely broken down.

The soldiers doing the fighting were mostly young children with no central command or organization. Young boys with guns roamed the land, trying to coerce other children to fight with them and killing everyone who got in their way. Some parents willingly sent their children to join the revolution and become soldiers. When children became soldiers, it meant protection for the family and a way for them to get food, which came from looting.

When the war began, only two rebel factions fought the government, but that number increased to six by the end of the conflict. It was difficult to know who was fighting whom and for what. The rebel soldiers had no uniforms although some factions wore identifying bandannas. The fighters were not paid; they were fighting for freedom. They paid themselves by looting the villages they attacked. Some factions were more brutal than others. Diamonds and gold from the mines were sold on the black market to import more guns to arm the rebels. Each soldier was given a gun. A strict curfew was enforced by whoever controlled a particular area—the government or the rebel soldiers—forcing people to become isolated in their houses.

By 1990 my village was feeling the effects of the war. People who lived inside the fenced areas had protection, but our village outside had none. Schools closed; widespread looting ravaged the country so trucks stopped delivering merchandise and food, and the stores were forced to shut down. Starvation had spread nationwide. The curfews even kept us from fishing because we fished at night.

One day three other boys and I decided to go fishing anyway. I was about twelve years old, and as the oldest child in my family I was expected to help provide for my siblings and our parents. The fish were to feed my family and use as barter for other things we needed. I had been fishing at the river many times before the war. We went on back roads because the main roads were unsafe. We carried handmade fishing poles, worms in a cup and empty rice bags for the fish. It was a four-hour walk to the river. We fished at night, paddling a canoe to the center of the river and setting out lines. The fish were tied to a rope in the water to keep them alive as long as possible before we started the four-hour walk back to the village.

On the way back we carried the fish we had caught in rice bags. When we were about forty-five minutes from home, rebel fighters stopped us with automatic weapons. Most of the twenty or twenty-five soldiers were young boys. They had guns, grenades and bombs. The soldiers had stretched a rope across the road and set up a checkpoint. They used human skulls and bodies as a barricade, spearing the bodies with pointed sticks and propping them up in a row like a fence. These dead bodies were meant as a warning. The soldiers stopped us some distance from the checkpoint, and three of them walked toward us. They told us to advance to be recognized. We told them we were going to the village behind them. They told us the village had been captured, and we couldn't go there because it was considered an enemy zone.

We were forced to join other people in line. We knew the soldiers belonged to a rebel faction because they didn't have uniforms. Everyone in line was aware of the danger we faced: girls were taken as sex slaves and cooks; boys were forced to fight in the revolution; small children were released or killed; and many adults were killed because they were thought to be part of the problem.

When our turn came they told us, "We are freedom fighters fighting a war and have come to liberate you. We've been fighting for a year. During this time we have never been fishing, and yet you have time to go fishing. You are not too young to fight, and we want you to join us."

We knew that no neutral ground existed with the soldiers. Asking us to join them was not a request. We were either with them or against them, and being against them meant death. The soldiers had captured all of the people walking on the road and made them get into three groups: men, women and children. Wives were separated from husbands; children were taken from their mothers and fathers. The soldiers needed the men and boys to fight and the women and girls to follow and cook for them wherever they went on the battlefields. They told us they were going to ask each of us if we were with them or against them. Each person would be asked individually to make a decision. If we refused to go with them, we knew we would be killed on the spot.

Before questioning us, they made us crawl by our elbows back and forth across the hard ground, scraping the skin from our arms. After that, they lashed our backs with electric cables cut from streetlights. Before lashing us, they dipped the cables in water and sand so they would scrape across our backs. Then they made us drag dead bodies from the streets into holes and ditches to be buried. Some of the bodies had decayed or were foul-smelling because of the chemicals used to kill them, but we were not allowed to wear a bandanna over our faces or hold our noses.

Then they talked to each of us. When it was my turn, they asked me what my name was. My family had always called me Willise, but I was afraid to tell my name for fear they would identify my tribe. I knew that many people in my tribe and family had worked for the government, and they would have been considered enemies to the rebels. I decided to use the name of a friend I had stayed with when I was in school back in Bong Mines—Eric.

The soldiers wanted me to fight alongside them because they needed boys like me. I told them I didn't know if I wanted to fight. I don't know what made me say that. The soldiers immediately threw me face down on the ground and pulled my arms behind my back until my elbows touched in the back, tying them tightly together. They also tied my legs. My chest was pulled so tight that I could feel the ropes cutting off my blood circulation and digging into my skin. My back and arms were bleeding. They threw me, along with about twenty other boys, into an empty house they were using for a prison. Everybody's life was in the hands of these children because they had the guns.

After two days the soldiers became nervous. Rumors were spreading that another rebel faction in the area was moving toward their location.

They decided it was time to move away, but they came to me one more time and asked if I was with them or against them. Did I want to live and fight, or die for nothing? This time I said I would fight, but when they untied my arms I couldn't move them. By this time the ropes had penetrated my flesh and cut off my blood circulation, causing my arms to be paralyzed and bent at the elbows. The soldier questioning me pointed to a gun on the ground and told me to pick it up. I couldn't do it. My hands and arms wouldn't move. He thought I was faking it and stabbed me in my arm to see if I could feel any pain. I couldn't feel anything. My paralyzed arms made me useless to them and anyone else, including me. The soldiers warned me not to return to my home, and then they left me to die.

5

The Lost Years Of My Life

Somehow I managed to get on my feet and leave the checkpoint. I followed a group of people of all ages and genders. We headed away from everything I knew. No one knew where we were going, but we knew we were safer in a group. People in the group helped me as we all walked together. We walked wherever our feet would take us. We ate stalks of sugar cane we found in the fields and on the roads. Along the way we had to go through many checkpoints manned by neighborhood militias. We walked for a week before finding a camp for displaced people in Kakata. I still couldn't move my arms, and they continued to be numb.

The camp in Kakata was housed in the Booker T. Washington Institute, a college about seventy miles from Monrovia. The school buildings had become accommodations for refugees. We slept on concrete floors or out-side in tents. Everyone was uneasy because fighting went on all around us.

At the camp we had to wait in line for hours to get a bowl of food from the single kitchen that fed us one meal a day. I was hungry and determined to stay in line until I reached the kitchen. When I got to the kitchen, a Red Cross worker from Switzerland saw I couldn't use my arms and couldn't carry a bowl or feed myself. She felt sorry for me and pulled me out of the line and asked someone to help me eat. She said she would talk to me when she finished feeding the hundreds of refugees in line. She knew I needed medical attention, but there was no medical help at the camp. All the Red Cross was allowed to do was provide basic food and shelter for the war victims.

The Red Cross worker decided to help me and several other children get out of the country. She swore us to secrecy and hid us in the back of a truck behind bags of rice and other supplies. She told us not to talk or make any noise no matter what happened. Seven trucks in the convoy headed toward Ivory Coast on the border with Liberia. Once again we came to many checkpoints. At some checkpoints soldiers demanded that all the goods be taken out of the trucks. Each time the Red Cross worker managed to convince the soldiers not to unload.

We drove through Central Liberia until finally the trucks reached Gbarnga, Bong County, Central Liberia, which was the headquarters for Rebel leader Charles Taylor, head of the largest rebel movement. Mr. Taylor signed the papers allowing the convoy to cross the border into Ivory Coast, a French-speaking country next to Liberia. Once we crossed into Ivory Coast, the Red Cross worker let us out of the truck and told us we were on our own. It was against international law for her to go beyond the border checkpoint. French soldiers stood at the border along with many refugees. We were in safe territory at this point, but we had to find our own help.

In the neighboring country of Ivory Coast, I walked to Danane, a major border town near Liberia which had a refugee reception center. Once there, I went to a police station with Red Cross and United Nations offices and asked for help.

6

Life In The Refugee Camp

When I first arrived at the camp, I had to register with both the government and the United Nations Refugee Agency. Lots of people were waiting in the hot sun. When it was my turn, they asked my name and age. I didn't know my age. No one had ever asked me any questions about it before. They told me to come up with a birthdate because they had to write down something on paper. I talked about this with others in the camp. Some people knew of the Chinese zodiac, so we looked at it to determine what year would be most like me. I picked a day and year: August 22, 1974, the Year of the Tiger.

I went back to the registration area and told the people that date. Then they asked who had brought me to the camp. I said no one. They helped me fill out a Red Cross Family Tracing Form listing the last place I had seen my family, our home address in Liberia and a description of my house. They labeled me as an "unaccompanied minor" and said I needed supervision. Before they could officially register me in the camp, an adult had to claim responsibility for me. They took my picture and posted it on a bulletin board with hundreds of other children who were unaccompanied and unidentified. They told me to stay around the camp and wait.

The camp at Danane had no hospital, and because having paralyzed arms was not considered a medical emergency I didn't receive any medical help. The nearest hospital was owned by the government, and it wasn't free. Although international and local volunteer doctors visited the camp, most already had a full list of patients and didn't have time to see anyone new. There was a long waiting time to see a doctor. When someone became very ill, three or four men carried the patient to the hospital on a makeshift litter. If a family member was not present to claim responsibility for the patient, the men were turned away, and the patient had to be carried back to the camp. People died with no family members to notify. The camp had deadly diseases; typhoid, dysentery and malaria killed many.

More than thirty thousand people lived in the camp in Danane. All of them needed food and shelter, and many needed medical attention. Tents measuring about six feet by ten feet and holding five or more people were everywhere. Each group of five only had one tent, and it had to last. During the rainy season, about six months out of the year, rainwater flowed into the tents and turned the dirt floors into mud. The water was sometimes so deep that we had to stand up. We couldn't sleep. In the dry season, the strong rays from the sun made the tent material deteriorate. When windstorms blew through the camp, people had to hold the tents down to keep them from flying away.

After a few weeks I got a call to go to the United Nations and Red Cross office building. The camp had no public address system or electricity. Someone holding a megaphone and walking through the camp made announcements. When I heard my name called, I went to the office. I met with Red Cross officials, and they said they had been sharing my story with the public but couldn't find any information about my parents.

Representatives from the Red Cross had gone back to Liberia and searched my village; but all the original inhabitants of the place were gone, and no one lived there anymore.

They said a lady by the name of Ms. Tenneh Howard had read my story and wanted to help me. She wanted me to stay in her tent and help with her three young children. The Red Cross would give her my food rations, and in return she would give me shelter and food. Once a month we got about three kilograms of rice, two kilograms of beans and two liters of oil per refugee. We were also given a rubber mat, a rubber bucket and a plastic cup, bowl and spoon. That was everything I had in the world to my name.

The camp was broken into segments labeled alphabetically. When meals were available from the one kitchen, each area was called in turn to get food. Water was distributed from a big tanker truck that showed up about once or twice a week. Whenever an announcement was made that the truck was in the camp, refugees lined up for miles with water buckets. Each person received one bucket of water to last an entire week. We had to decide how best to use the water: drinking, cooking, bathing or washing clothes.

There were big food distribution sites. Cans of food were labeled with letters corresponding with letters for the various groups in the refugee camp. Sometimes we sold our food rations. We also learned how to fake the letters in order to get extra food, which we sold to the citizens out-side the camp.

A community-based school had mostly adult refugee teachers. I attended the Protestant Methodist School for refugees in Danane for a couple of years.

One day during the rainy season Ms. Tenneh was struggling with the tent, trying hard to keep it from being blown away by the storm. I felt sorry for her, but I couldn't help her because my arms were bent at the elbows and I couldn't move them. She found a kitchen knife and told me to follow her. We went into a forest area, and she cut a long piece of bamboo tree into pieces the length of my arms. She smoothed them out. Then she forcibly straightened both my arms and tied each arm to a bamboo splint. It didn't hurt because I still had no feeling in my arms. Every evening she removed the ropes and splints. She boiled water and massaged my arms with warm mud and then put the splints back on. I never saw a doctor or had therapy. After about three months I started feeling some pain. She said that was good and it meant my body was healing itself, and she was right. In time, my arms healed completely.

I couldn't stay in the camp in Danane because it was too close to Liberia. Rebel soldiers began crossing the borders at night, invading the camps and killing people and then running back to Liberia. I had to leave, so I decided to walk to the Republic of Ghana, where English is the national language.

7

Christmas In The Refugee Camp

Guinea Republic

Crossing borders in Africa was difficult. I didn't have a passport or any other form of identification because I had left Liberia with nothing but the clothes on my back. I walked with a group of boys, and people were naturally suspicious of teenage boys. At the border were military checkpoints with soldiers to enforce laws about immigration and customs. I couldn't just walk through, but I found a method that helped me cross. I stayed at the border for a few days and watched the activities of the local people. I noticed that every morning at 6:30 the border opened for about thirty or forty-five minutes and allowed merchants to go back and forth with goods between the two countries before the barricades were put back up. The merchants often had their children walking with them and carrying items to sell or trade. I waited for morning, and when I saw a family getting ready to cross I walked near them and pretended to be part of the family. I tried this method at several border crossings; sometimes it took me a week to find the right group to cross with. I knew if I were caught I would go to jail.

I reached a camp in the Republic of Guinea around Christmas. We heard people talking about God, but we were always angry and didn't want to listen. We were especially angry with Christians and religious people for talking about how God is love and will take care of His children and how He loves the poor, as well as the weak and oppressed. How do you explain this to someone who has lost everything, including their parents? But December was the best time to be in a refugee camp because this was the month of the year when various Christian denominations came to the camps with food, relief materials and medication to distribute to the refugees. They brought truckloads of food and other supplies that lasted for a couple of weeks, normally from December 15 through the thirtieth of the month, and then, as we refugees said, "Christ is gone, and the crisis is back."

In 1992 the Red Cross and the United Nations High Commissioner for Refugees announced a shortage of food for refugees. We would have no extra food distribution in December because donor countries did not give enough supplies for every refugee to receive something. The only food available was to be given to those who were the most vulnerable, children ages one to ten and the elderly. Those in-between were left out, causing us to become frustrated and angry. Once in a while, pastors I described as radicals for Christ would come to the refugee camp to talk to us about Christ and His love and compassion for the refugees, but we didn't pay attention to them.

8

Nothing But Hope

I n 1992, a couple of days before Christmas in the refugee camp, a pastor started preaching with a bullhorn or megaphone. He was walking around the camp preaching around 4 a.m.. This was pretty smart because it was about the only time people might be listening and not be out looking for food or water. We were all sleeping on dirt floors in our tent when we heard his voice. I was partially asleep, but something he said woke me up. He said: "God has blessed you and spared your lives to live another year. How did you escape the war? How fast were you? How smart were you? How skillful were you? What saved you? Where are your parents, friends, the government, the UN or even the U.S. and Liberian governments? Where are those you trusted who you thought would save you? God has a plan and a purpose for your life. Some of you will return to your homes like the prophet Nehemiah returned to rebuild the walls. Many of you will return as change agents. Are you going into the new year with an old attitude with God? With anger and bitterness? Or is it time to surrender and accept God?"

He asked questions I couldn't answer. The preacher then said, "If you believe me and what I have said from the Bible, then I want to pray for you. Close your eyes wherever you are, and I will pray for you." I closed my eyes in my tent, lying down on a dirt floor, and prayed with him for the very first time in my life.

He said the sinner's prayer for me. "I don't have a Bible, food or anything to give you," he said, "but God has a way of giving you what you need. Find other Christians in the refugee camp to help you with your new walk in Christ and stay focused on Jesus, and He will take you places you never imagined possible."

I never got out of my tent to see that man's face, but he led me to God and helped change my life forever. This preacher probably went home feeling disappointed that he spent several hours preaching without one single person coming out to him in person to receive Christ. But I heard his message that beautiful morning, and my life has never been the same.

The next day I went to see a friend who had grown up in the home of former Baptist missionaries in Nimba County in the north central part of Liberia. He had a hymnbook he used to sing and read about God. His name was Emmanuel, and he knew a lot about the Bible from the missionaries. The missionary family had taken him in but had to leave him behind at the mission camp when the war started because there was no legal paperwork to help him leave Africa.

9

Buduburam Refugee Camp

Republic Of Ghana

I sold food from the camp in Guinea to earn money so I could go on to Ghana. I traveled with a group of boys. Whenever refugees left the camp in both Ivory Coast and Guinea, they were supposed to check in with the local police station to fill out a form, which was written in French. This was to help control the movement of refugees in the country. When I left the camp, I didn't go to the police station to get the pass because I didn't know exactly where I was going. I was about thirteen or fourteen years old.

For a while we travelled from town to town between Ghana, Togo and Benin with plans to go farther north. Sometimes we hitched a ride; sometimes we walked, while at other times we rode the bus. None of us had identification. We were young boys the same age as many of the soldiers in Liberia and had no adult supervision. We slept on the beach and under bridges, begging for money to pay for food and a bus ticket to the next town. I had no idea where I was going, but I knew what I was running away from. We thought eventually we would cross over into Europe—making plans although we had no passports. The farther we got away from Liberia, the more sympathetic people were to us. By that time, people in countries closer to Liberia were tired of the war and all the refugee crises. Many times I was stopped and thrown into jail because no one knew what to do with me. I eventually learned that if I went to the roughest part of town I could hide and sometimes get help. At each border the authorities asked for documents, but I didn't have any. Usually I was able to sneak across.

One day I reached a camp called Buduburam in the suburb of Accra, the capital of Ghana in West Africa. Tens of thousands of refugees were in the camp along with a police station. They sent me to the Liberian Refugees Welfare Council in the camp. A Red Cross coordinator by the name of Mr. Kofi was in charge of unaccompanied minors. The late Pope John Paul II had built a special housing unit with three homes for orphans and a school for refugees. A public school called Buduburam Junior Secondary School was located in a village adjacent to the refugee camp. Chairman Momo of the Liberian Refugees Welfare Council and his family were in charge of the orphans and unaccompanied children. Chairman Momo's mother and his sister, Ms.Teta, were the two energetic and concerned ladies who took good care of us and kept every one of us in line. The Red Cross paid the fees for the school on my behalf. The Catholic Church and many other refugee agencies provided food and clothes, with special care for the elderly and minor children. The farther I was from Liberia, the better I was received and treated.

I finally got a Bible in Ghana, an English-speaking country. I didn't know anything about faith, grace, forgiveness, humility and empathy. Through the Bible I learned about taking care of others and forgiving those who had hurt me. My Christian education took place over time, but once I became a Christian I was vocal and proactive. The Bible helped me get through the healing process without being consumed by anger, grief and a desire for revenge.

One day we were told the Red Cross funds for our program had run out. They brought all of us to the Osu Children's Home in Accra. The home belonged to the Orphanage Support Services Organization. Upon our arrival each of us was taken to a room for counseling. They asked me if I was an orphan. I said I didn't think so. Then they told me that if I wasn't an orphan I wouldn't fit into their program. It was specifically designed to take care of orphans who would be sent away to live in other countries far from their home country. I knew this would take me farther from my home, so I didn't want to be part of the program. I told them I was not an orphan. I was then taken back to the refugee camp, but with the cuts in funding and shortage of food I couldn't stay. I had to move on.

The educational programs inside the refugee camps were community-based. Sometimes people in the camp taught school classes, but we had no stability. The primary concern of the various refugee and relief agencies was to provide a little bit of food, shelter and basic medicine. Education was not considered a priority because the need for basic services was overwhelming. I was frustrated.

For years I moved from camp to camp. I eventually ended up in the Oru-Ijebu refugee camp in Ogun State, Nigeria, West Africa.

10

Oru Refugee Camp

Federal Republic Of Nigeria

Oru Refugee Camp was in Ogun State in southwest Nigeria. Once again many refugees were there, and food was scarce. People resorted to stealing. Many of the girls and women became prostitutes just to get money to survive. Sometimes they were raped; many were killed. Men became armed robbers and thieves. I was hungry, so I joined others stealing for food. We stole produce from farms on the weekends when the farmers were away—bananas, pineapples, oranges, cassava. We also caught goats and chickens and brought them back to our tents. The farmers were very angry and threatened us with voodoo spells and death. It is easy to think of the farmers as being the victims, but they were part of the problem. Some of them hired refugees to help on their farms but paid them little or nothing. The farms were far away from the camp. We had to walk two to three hours just to get there and then work all day. Only one meal was provided. Often at the end of the day the farmer disappeared and never paid us. We then had to find our way back to the camp. We didn't speak the language and always faced the danger of being picked up by police. The police would not investigate the farmers unless we paid them. Many people took advantage of us, and we became rogues and thieves out of necessity.

I realized even then that stealing was wrong, but we had no choice because we were starving to death. We had no immediate hope of surviving unless we did something. Looking back at my actions today I have guilty feelings, realizing these farmers worked very hard, and we would come in and steal their crops and farm produce.

Every day we faced physical and emotional barriers. Most refugees were angry, with a lot of bitterness, hurt and desire for revenge. We were so influenced by what was going on in our environment. When you've seen this much trouble and death, you become desensitized. There is no good versus evil; you constantly see evil. We were always in survival mode, thinking only about how to get through that day. We sat around campfires at night and talked. Rumors spread about the U.S. government family reunion program that allowed Liberian families living in the U.S. to bring over their relatives who were still in Liberia or exiled in refugee camps. We learned most of our news around the camp through rumors and speculations.

11

My Journey To Lagos, Nigeria

Earlier in my wandering days back in 1990, I had met a Nigerian peacekeeper soldier in Liberia named Tues Tokunbo. We became friends, and he gave me his name and address in Nigeria in case I ever needed it. In 2001 the living conditions in our Nigerian refugee camp were terrible. I became disillusioned about life, and then I remembered having his address. I decided to see if he could help me. The address was in Lagos, the capital of Nigeria. I stole food and sold it to get the money for a bus ticket to Lagos. I had only enough money for a one-way ticket. In my mind I thought I would find him and he would help me buy a return ticket.

I found the address he had given me, but he wasn't there. I asked local people if they knew him, but no one did. Then I saw a woman selling bags of chips and food outside the address and asked her if she knew him. She did, and she told me he had moved away. She said he was in the Nigerian Navy and had been reposted years ago in the northern part of the country. I was now alone in a city of fourteen million, and at that time it was a very violent city. I needed money to get a ticket back to the refugee camp. The woman couldn't help me; she thought I was fortunate to be in a camp where they gave me food and shelter free of charge. She said she had to find her own food and shelter as a Nigerian citizen. "I am living in my own country worse than a refugee," she said. The woman told me to try begging from other people in the streets for help, but she warned me that people were suspicious of strangers. One man finally helped me and gave me twenty naira (currency in Nigeria). "This will get you part of the way," he said.

I arrived at the bus station around 5 or 6 p.m. I went to the office of the public transport vehicles union to see if someone could help me get back to the camp. A man told me to talk to the driver of the last bus for the day. I found him, only to find out the seats were oversold. The bus driver got me on another bus that would take me about an hour out of town. He said I might be able to get a free bus ticket to the camp from there. I got on that bus which was also overloaded, and it was held up in traffic for more than two hours. When we arrived at the next bus station in Ikorodu Town in Lagos State, Nigeria, the last bus for the night heading to the Oru Refugee Camp was already on its way. I could see it from a distance with the smoke coming out of the exhaust pipe.

The city was filled with chaos, and I knew my life was in danger because of the violence. I was a teenage boy with no identification. I looked for someone else who would help me. People warned me that vigilantes watched over the city at night and killed suspicious persons who were out on the street. Someone told me my only hope was to go to a mosque and stay there for the night. I found a mosque and spoke to the imam. He said he didn't want troublemakers in the mosque and turned me away. People had approached him before and stolen the shoes and other footwear the worshippers left at the door while they were praying.

I went to the police station to explain my story. "Do you see a sign here that says Hotel for Refugees?" a policeman asked. "The only place we have for you to stay is the jail. I can put you in jail and release you tomorrow." I walked outside to think about that. I didn't want to be in jail, but I knew I needed a place to stay for the night.

I saw a lady selling food in front of the police station and told her what they had said. "Don't be fooled," she said. "If you go into the jail they won't release you easily. Christian churches are nearby. Christ Apostolic is a fifteen-minute walk from here. Try to sleep there."

I walked to the church. The entrance was behind a metal locked gate. A guard at the gate turned me away because I didn't have a church membership ID card. I insisted on seeing the pastor in charge. Finally the pastor came out and talked to me through the steel gate. He told me no one in the city was supposed to be out after curfew, which began in fifteen minutes. He told me to come back in a few days on a worship day when the treasurer, charity committee and board members would be in church. He said no money was kept in the church. I was stunned because I was not asking for money; I just needed a place to spend the night, and then I would be gone the next day.

As I turned to go back to the police station I heard the bell tolling for curfew. I was afraid. I knew it was dangerous to be out, so I ran into an empty building under construction. Before long I fell asleep. Around 3 a.m. I was awakened with a bright light in my face. I was surrounded by vigilantes. They had daggers and spoke in the Hausa language from the north of the country. "We're going to kill you," they said. They didn't believe I was from a refugee camp because they couldn't imagine a refugee leaving a camp that had food and shelter. They beat me and dragged me out in the streets and then finally brought me to the town square, or roundabout, of Ikorodu Town. Vigilantes typically took captives there. Often they would then tie them up, drop car tires over them, pour gasoline on the tires and set them on fire. If anyone asked questions, the vigilantes claimed the victim was an armed robber.

I was beaten and taken to the square about 4 a.m. People came out to see the troublemaker who had been caught. They were happy someone was finally caught, and it wasn't hard to stir up anger in the crowd. For the first time I was certain I was going to die. I was in a place with strange people, a strange language, no friends and seemingly no escape. The vigilantes tied me up and threw tires over me. A crowd gathered to watch and jeer.

At around 5:30 a.m. a lady who had been praying in a church over-night—what we called an overnight church service—came up, forced her way through the crowd and asked if I was an armed robber.

I said, "No."

"What is your faith?"

"I'm a Christian."

She then said, "What's happening tonight is between you and your God."

I prayed, "God, I think You can save me."

The lady told me she had a brother who used to be a peacekeeper in Liberia. She said she would try to find him when she got home and see if he could help me. And then she left.

After a while I heard a gunshot. The military police arrived in the square. A man in charge of the patrol asked me if I was an armed robber. I told him my story, but he didn't believe me. I learned this was the lady's brother who had served in Liberia in the 1990s. My last chance was to convince him I was a Liberian refugee. I began speaking to him in Liberian English. He asked me questions, and my answers convinced him I was from Liberia. I was taken to another police station and thrown into jail to await trial. No one knew where I was.

About twenty-five to thirty inmates were in the jail. We had no electricity. The inmates stripped me of my clothes. We slept on a concrete floor. In jail I learned a lot about how the government was run from the inmates. Fees were levied for everything. In the prison, fees were to be paid to the government for toilets and housing. Every evening we shared stories, one person at a time. When I finished my story, they were all in tears. One of the leaders said, "You have a compelling story. It could have been me." Many of us became friends and exchanged addresses to use after we got out. I had about six addresses. In time I became the leader of the group in prison.

I waited six months in jail. The police refused to help me by contacting the refugee camp to check my identification or just to let them know I was in prison. Their thought was, if you're not important enough for them to find you, why should we care? The man in charge of my case said, "I can't release you. It would cause trouble in the community because they think you're a robber who had terrorized them for years. I have to wait until the owner of the building in which you were caught returns to Nigeria from abroad to verify your story; the house owner will have to decide your case, whether you go to court or not."

Finally the woman who owned the building returned to the country from England, driving a Rolls Royce. "If you want to be free, give me the names of your collaborators," she demanded. I had no names to give. She was angry and sent me back to jail because she thought I was guilty.

One day the commissioner of police was passing through town and stopped by the police station for a brief visit. He talked with the prisoners. He asked each of us our name and offense. He saw my name was not on the prisoners' list and asked me to explain my story. He said I needed to go to court because six months was too long to be waiting in jail. He set a court date for one week later. One prisoner overheard and told me to be encouraged with this news. "All of us will die one day; you just know the day," he said. "Some of us go early, some later. The real judge is God who we should all be afraid of."

The next week I was taken to court in chains like a hardened criminal. The judge told me I was guilty until proven innocent—that was the law in Nigeria, but I couldn't understand that law because in Liberia you are considered innocent until proven guilty. "Are you sure you're a refugee from Liberia?" she asked. She listened to my story and then sent me back to jail. She said she would try to establish my identity first before proceeding with the case. I waited in jail for two weeks. The judge discovered the United Nations had a file on me with a picture ID. Because of this she released me on parole. I had to return to the court every Friday. I used the addresses from the prisoners to find a place to stay in Lagos so I could go back to court each Friday. I returned to the judge four times, and then she released me from parole. "What's your plan?" she asked.

"I want to go to school," I said. She told me to find a technical school—something not too expensive. Such a school was near the refugee camp. The judge paid my tuition. She told me I reminded her of her own son and daughter who were living in the United Kingdom and the United States, working and studying in foreign lands.

"Who knows what situation they could be in if they were in a strange city?" she said. "Come see me every month, and I will give you food." I went to school for three and a half years in Nigeria through her support.

A few years later, after my studies at the technical college, I was offered an opportunity to attend the Archbishop Benson Idahosa All Nations for Christ Bible Institute. One day I went to House on the Rock Church in Lagos led by Pastor Paul Adefarasin. I wanted to talk with the Liberian pastor, Tugbeh Jackson, who was serving there, to seek financial support from him to sustain myself in the Bible school and meet my needs in the refugee camp. Pastor Jackson was the musical director of the church and a former student himself from the All Nations for Christ Bible Institute in Benin City, Nigeria. But they were too busy to talk with me that day.

As I was standing in the lobby area I started talking with Mr. Desmond Ovbiagle, a Nigerian banker at City Bank. He was not a member of the church but was just visiting. I told him I lived in Oru Refugee Camp near Lagos and had been there for years. The banker was shocked to hear a camp was near Lagos. He said he didn't have any money with him, but he wanted to hear more of my story. He asked me to meet him at a restaurant in Victoria Island at noon the following day. It was my first time to eat at a restaurant. We became friends, and he gave me five thousand Nigerian naira. Almost overnight I had monetary support from this strange man who didn't know me at all. Desmond was moved with compassion to support me regularly both in and out of school throughout my remaining years in Nigeria. He helped me live a much more decent life in the refugee camp. God used him to change the course of my life completely and put me on a brand new path.

12

The 842 Computer Training Center

About a year later around Christmas, after I first met with Desmond and was enjoying a wonderful relationship with him, he decided to visit the refugee camp where I lived. One day I rode with him in his company car three hours to the refugee camp. When we got there he asked me, "What do all the young people do each day? Do you go to church?" I told him we had a pastor from Sierra Leone who was a refugee herself. She ran one of the churches for the refugees in the camp and prayed with us. He wanted to know if we had materials, like Bibles and other Christian literature.

At a later date, Desmond gave me about ten bags of rice to give to Pastor Aisha Massaquoi, the spiritual head of our church in the refugee camp. He also bought her a drum set and some music and gospel materials. He gave me fifty thousand naira, about five hundred dollars U.S., and told me to give it to the pastor. He prayed for God's blessing upon me. I gave the rice, generator, money and other materials to Pastor Aisha, and she wrote a letter of appreciation to Desmond.

I was ordained a deacon in the church at once. After I finished school, Desmond asked me what I wanted to do next with my life while I was waiting for the day to return home to Liberia. I said I wanted to go to school again to learn about computers. About thirty minutes away was a school I wanted to attend, called Lagos City Computer College, but Desmond thought the best thing would be for me to learn on a personal computer at home in the camp. He said he would get a computer for me.

In 2002 Mr. Edward Tamba was the first Liberian refugee who had learned how to use a computer and was actually lecturing at the Lagos City Computer College. He had studied computer science in college in Nigeria. Desmond gave me a computer and paid Edward Tamba to teach me for six to eight weeks. The computer was a Windows XP multi-media system fully loaded with tutorials to help me learn faster. My learning time with Mr. Tamba was from 6 to 8 p.m., Monday through Friday. In no time I had learned the history of the computer, PowerPoint, Windows XP and other things. I learned in my room, which was in a concrete building with a small power generator. Other refugees lined up to watch us in my computer class.

All of a sudden I felt like Donald Trump or Bill Gates in the camp. I became the richest man in the refugee camp overnight. I was the only refugee who had a computer and private generator and an opportunity to acquire a skill and earn money at the same time to take care of my needs. One day I had an idea. I thought about the fact that I had gained so much, and to whom much is given, much is expected. We have been blessed to be a blessing to others, according to the Bible. I thought this knowledge had been given to me so I could pass it on. I felt this one computer had a purpose: for me to give back by teaching others and investing in my community.

One day a refugee from Liberia, the late Mr. Henry Toe, came to see me and asked me to train his young son, James Toe, on the computer. That was my beginning. I designed a brochure for a computer school in camp. One hundred refugees signed up within the first week of registration. We had that one computer set up on a table in my room, and the refugees lined up to learn. Each refugee was given five minutes of training time to learn how to hold and move the mouse, turn the computer on and learn the names of the various parts of the computer. Then it was the next refugee's turn.

I was amazed to see how many people wanted this experience. It gave them something to do, something new to learn. I began feeling the pressure to take the computer out of my room so I could teach more refugees. I wanted women to learn too, and they didn't feel free to come into a man's room to learn.

I returned to Lagos to ask Desmond to come and see what was happening. When he came, refugees were lined up sitting in the hot sun just waiting to touch that one computer.

In the midst of all this I had applied for relocation to Australia through an Australian offshore humanitarian visa (Australian Immigration Form 842). A refugee friend who had travelled to Australia told me about this opportunity and told me to look it up on the Internet. This was the first time I had heard of the Internet. I went to Desmond's office and asked him to help me find Form 842 on the Internet and to print some copies for me. I filled out one of the forms, mailed it out and waited. About three weeks later I got a response. It was the first letter I had ever received. It was an official letter from the Australian Embassy saying my application was received and was being processed in the order in which it was received. Everyone knew I had received that letter, and they all wanted to apply.

That gave me the idea to sell the forms and use the money to purchase materials to build a school at the camp. I announced to other refugees that for the price of making fifty to one hundred mud bricks I would give them a form. I explained that the bricks would be used to build the walls of the new computer center. Everyone was excited about this plan. James Toe became the business director, and I became the unofficial Australian High Commissioner in the camp. We built the first school from foundation to roof using those mud bricks. Desmond saw this and said he would pay for the roof and fund the completion of the building as well as donate two more computers. He also donated another small portable generator to boost the electricity supply to the center.

The school was so impressive that it inspired others to ask what we needed. By 2005 we had seventeen computers. Then we built another building that was able to hold five hundred students. They came from all over Africa: Sudan, Ethiopia, Sierra Leone and other regions.

One day the territorial commander, Stuart Mungate, of the Salvation Army in Nigeria was bringing in food and material supplies for the refugees. He was on his way out and stopped to talk with a little boy at the refugees' administrative building. The little boy asked, "When will you people stop bringing us food and clothes and bring us education?"

Commander Mungate said, "It is difficult to provide education in this kind of environment."

And then the little boy asked, "If we had our own school in the camp, would you support it?"

The commander said yes. The little boy then took the commander to the other end of the refugee camp and showed him our computer school with seventeen computers but not enough electricity to run the school. The commander was so stunned he gave the boy a business card and asked him to give it to the person in charge of the school.

After my return to the camp I got the business card and went to see the commander at the Salvation Army Territorial Headquarters in Lagos. I explained to him that I thought one of the causes of the war in Liberia and many other parts of Africa was because people were not educated. Therefore, they had no hope for the future, and that leads to bitterness and anger. "To fix this problem," I said, "we need education. We can't rebuild the country without skills and education. We must fight the darkness of the mind and the darkness of the heart altogether at the same time."

"What is your greatest need?" he asked me.

"A generator," I said.

"This is not part of the Salvation Army's mission to the camp, and it is not our initiative; therefore it is not in our budget. But I'm touched by your personal life story and sacrifices to help educate young people in a challenging environment like the camp," he said. "I'll buy a 6.5 kVA generator with my own money." He bought the generator, and the Salvation Army built the room for it and paid for the setup. Now that we had a reliable source of electricity we started training more people from the community.

Many refugees and Nigerian citizens trained on those computers went on to hold high positions of influence and offices in society, including Mr. Jerelimic Piah who became press secretary to Liberian President Ellen Johnson Sirleaf. Our first graduation was in 2005. Our school was called the 842 Computer Training Center in honor of the Australian Immigration Form 842, and it's still operating today, not in Nigeria in the refugee camp, but in Liberia.

I learned my visa request had been rejected by the Australian government because I had no one to host me. I had also applied for resettlement to the Canadian government but was rejected. I then decided to continue my focus on the computer center. I was honored by a women's group, Ultimate

Women Organization of Nigeria, for my contribution to women's education. In 2005 I was awarded the Rare Gems Humanitarian Award for my "relentless and sacrificial humanitarian efforts" in the refugee camp.

Shortly afterward, the Liberian civil war ended, and I began to develop a burning desire to get involved in finding solutions to the generational poverty facing my post-war nation. I felt I needed to return to my home country and help with the rebuilding process. I wanted to return to Liberia to give back that which I had received in the refugee camp in Nigeria by teaching young hopeless adults and children computer skills instead of giving them guns and drugs to kill people and destroy properties.

13

Taking The Vision To Liberia

I n 2005 Desmond bought an airline ticket for me to fly to Liberia for the first time in many years. This was my first time, and the first time for a member of my family, to fly on a plane. He gave me ten thousand U.S. dollars. "I trust you and believe in you," he said. "Do not look for money any more from now going onward. The most important resource any human being can have is integrity. Everything else in life is replaceable except credibility. You will succeed in life if you keep on being a man of integrity. Use the money I gave you the best way possible to purchase land and build the school to fulfill the vision God has given you and the burden He's given us for your country Liberia to expand the 842 Computer Training Center there."

I persuaded six other Liberian refugees who shared my passion and vision to return to Liberia as a team and positively impact the lives of the next generation through computer education. The team's other members were five men named Mr. Momo V. Ware, Mr. George A. Thomas, Pastor Kollie Jallah, Mr. Anderson Cherub and Mr. Ishaka Jumel Tutray, and one woman, Ms. Ramatu Freeman aka Redeemed. We went to Liberia, bought one acre of land in the City View, Rehab Community area, in lower Johnsonville, Montserrado County, and built the first computer training center there. It was hard work, but our memories of hacking down the jungle and driving out the monkeys and snakes make us laugh today.

Desmond is really the godfather of Change Agent Network and the most influential person in my life. He changed the trajectory of my life completely when I was a confused, lost and forgotten young man in the refugee camp. He changed my worldview, built and strengthened my faith in God. He gave me a new identity and assisted me in discovering my purpose and fulfilling it. I honestly don't know what would have become of my life if Desmond had not allowed God to use him in rescuing me. He taught me biblical values and principles over material and monetary gains and success. Desmond till this day remains the number one investor in my personal life and assignment. The most humbling thing about our relationship is that Desmond has never been to Liberia. He has invested tens of thousands of dollars in Liberia but has never been there himself. Oh, it is just God!

I was working in Liberia one day when my phone rang. It was someone from the refugee camp in Nigeria saying my name was included in information placed on the bulletin board to travel to the United States. The Nigerian government and the various refugee agencies were considering shutting down the camp, but they had to repatriate refugees to their various home countries. They helped some of the refugees locally integrate into the Nigerian society, and a small percentage was to be resettled among the developed nations of the world. Soon I heard that an immigration team from the U.S. had selected me to be resettled to America, but I didn't want to go. I had taken money from people in good faith to build a school in Liberia for children and young people, and I felt that I had to finish the project at all costs and set it up properly before I could go anywhere, including America.

I said I couldn't leave Liberia to return to Nigeria to go through the resettlement process at that time. The person I spoke with at the United Nations High Commissioner for Refugees office in Lagos said I was the most honest refugee she had ever met. "Most refugees, upon receiving information like this about traveling abroad to the developed world, would lie and do whatever they could to travel to the U.S. By telling me this, you are telling me you are not afraid to be in Liberia, and this would ordinarily disqualify you from the U.S. resettlement program. This is because the program is only designed and set up for refugees who cannot return to their home country because of insecurity and death threats to their lives. But you don't have any of these concerns. Come back in three months, and I'll help you requalify and go through the process. I believe you will do a lot more amazing things for humanity and your country if you are given the opportunity to travel to the U.S.A."

In three months, after the project was finished, I told the people in Liberia I was going back to Nigeria and eventually traveling to the United States, but I would never forget them. I promised them I would find a way to send food and money to sustain the school until I could return.

I returned to Nigeria. I still wasn't sure if I should go to America because I was afraid if I left, the work I had started would stop and eventually die. One day before my return to Liberia, while I was still in Nigeria running the computer center, I went to Lagos to try to raise funds to support the computer education program in the camp. While I was gone, Martin Webb, a twenty-one-year-old graduate from England, showed up at the camp. He was in Nigeria on an exchange program with the British Council. He was a young filmmaker taking part in a documentary project looking at the importance of African border crossings and their meaning for the survival of refugees fleeing conflict.

After completing his project, he had two extra days at the end of his trip and decided he wanted to visit the refugee camp. As he walked around the camp he saw hunger, desperation and poverty everywhere. Many refugees were asking him, "White man, white man, what have you brought for us to eat? Did you bring some food, water or money for us? Take us with you to America." Little did they know that Martin Webb was not from America.

While touring the camp, Martin came across our 842 Computer Training Center. Our building was neat, organized and landscaped with beautiful flowers in the yard. This was in stark contrast to other buildings in the camp. He was shocked to see such a place in the middle of the refugee camp and asked what it was and who built it. Some of the refugees told him the computer school was a community–based, self-help initiative. They told him I had organized this self-help project. He was so impressed that he said he wanted to meet and talk to me and would wait for me to return from Lagos. I didn't get back until about eight or nine that evening.

As I walked through the main entrance of the camp, many refugees were waiting to tell me someone had come to see me. Most of them thought Martin was waiting to take me with him to England. When I met Martin he told me he was amazed that in a camp like this we were focused on providing education to refugees. Most of the refugees in this camp were only begging for food and money and thinking of how they would survive that day. I told him I was concerned we were not planning for the next generation. "What are we giving to them? How are we going to rebuild our country with no skills, no training and no hope? Education is so important, but in the camps the primary concern is providing food, shelter and medication until we have a more stable life. What I'm trying to do here is prepare the next generation for the challenges they will face when we eventually return to Liberia to rebuild a destroyed nation."

Martin asked how I could do that, and I said, "I don't know, but I have to start from somewhere." He said he had never heard anyone in such a situation talk like this before; if I ever decided to return to Liberia to fulfill my mission and vision, he would follow me to do a documentary film on my life. "You are too skinny," he told me. "I want to buy you some food to eat."

"I don't need food for myself," I told him. "But if you want to do something for me, buy some diesel fuel for the generator to run the computer center and teach computer skills to the refugees in the camp for the short time you are here."

Martin bought a drum of diesel and taught some classes for two days before returning to England. Martin Webb became our first white international volunteer. He filmed me in the camp that day and talked with other refugee volunteers. After he left, we exchanged e-mails and stayed in communication.

When I met Martin I didn't know what to think of him. It did not seem normal to me for a young white man to stay in the camp with me for two days. I had never seen anyone like him. I felt as if he was up to something, but I wasn't sure exactly what he wanted from me. Nobody outside of Africa had ever expressed much interest in my life and the work I did in this camp.

Questions about Martin kept going through my mind. I thought most people didn't care about someone unless they had ulterior motives. Why would he care about me so much that he was willing to risk his own life by being in the refugee camp? Why would a young man with no money or a real job spend two days with us in this camp volunteering at the school?

Why wasn't he concerned about his own safety? He was the only white man hanging out with a bunch of desperate refugees in the camp. Was it possible he had confidence in my work and vision for the future?

Martin was willing to do everything I asked him to do for the refugee community, and he did it with joy. I saw only love, honesty and genuine concern for my life and future in his eyes. His visit to the camp and my growing relationship with him helped me realize I was able to offer something significant to my society. He helped me know I had an important story to share with the world and that I could help shape the culture of the next generation of Liberians. He helped validate my story and helped me understand I had something very important to give to the world.

I was still uncertain about going to America on the refugee resettlement program. I was afraid my projects would die if I left them unattended. Rumors spread in the camp that once refugees got to the United States they were forced into the army and sent to Iraq or Afghanistan. I also seriously considered the issue of slavery in America and how that ugly situation had affected us all the way over in Liberia.

I sent an e-mail to Martin in England sharing these concerns with him. I wrote him because he is a Westerner, he lives there, and he knows what's going on there. He was the only true friend I had from the West. He encouraged me to go and said I would meet a lot of people who might be able to help me. He said I would have to make that decision for myself, but he would come to visit me in America if I decided to go.

14

New World: Lafayette, Louisiana

O ne day people from the immigration office at the U.S. Embassy arrived at the camp in black Chevy vans. I was still confused about why I was being offered a chance to go the United States. I hadn't applied to go there. I was told the refugee camps were being shut down now that there was peace in Liberia and several other countries. The various refugee agencies were planning to close the camp by helping the refugees integrate into their host nation, repatriate to their home country or resettle in developed nations of the world such as the United States, Canada and European countries. Refugee files and applications had been sent to other countries, so the countries could select whom to help. The United States selected me because my file included my work with the computer center. The U.S. Department of Immigration shared my file with churches and nonprofit organizations to determine which state and city would take me. According to the plan, the immigration office would give me legal documents to get me into the country, and then one of those churches or nonprofit organizations would help me with the resettlement process in their own town, city and state.

Refugees had to meet one of three criteria if they wanted to be resettled in the developed world. The first was that the refugee be what was called a long-stay refugee, someone who had continuously lived in the camp for more than a decade. The second was that the refugee had been tortured or abused with visible scars to prove it. The refugee was required to give names, dates and a description of what happened. I met these first two criteria for the program. The last was what they called women at risk. A specific resettlement program had been set up for single women with children who had been raped or abused and who had no one to support them.

I made the decision to go to the United States, but the idea of immigrating seemed unreal until I was taken to the U.S. Embassy for a medical exam and tests. While I was there I saw "LA" stamped on my documents as my final destination in America. I thought I was being sent to Los Angeles. Later I was surprised to learn that LA meant Louisiana, a state I knew nothing about. My faith was and is very important to me. It reminded me that everything would work out, even if I didn't know the outcome or have the details of what exactly was going on.

My departure date was August 27, 2006. The United Nations provided transportation to the airport for me and other refugees selected for resettlement. We were put on a Lufthansa flight although we didn't have passports or visas. A lady from the International Organization for Migration gave each of us a bag with IOM printed across the front. She told us to hold it in front of us but not to open or squeeze it. Before we boarded the flight, she told me to sign a promissory note to pay back the travel loan given to me by the Catholic Church for providing transportation to the United States. The note was for about three thousand dollars, which was to be paid back in three or four years. The IOM agent explained that this note would help me establish my first line of credit in the U.S.

"I can't go," I said. "This must be some kind of trick. There is no way I can pay that kind of money back; it is just too much. In Africa it is not normal for people to loan you money. We buy everything we need." She explained that the money to pay the note goes to help other refugees resettle. She said I shouldn't worry about it. It would be okay if I couldn't repay it. So I got on the plane.

The airplane was huge. People were talking, eating, drinking, reading; some were watching movies sitting in seats with headphones and laptops. People were smiling, and I didn't know why. It was a completely foreign world to me. I sat down and held my IOM bag in front of me. I felt as if I were among a bunch of aliens on a foreign planet during the five-hour flight.

I saw my first snow as we flew into Frankfurt Airport in Germany. When we got off the plane it was a complete culture shock. Our plane didn't go to the main arrival terminal, so we had to get off and board a bus that took us to the main terminal. It was freezing cold, and I had no jacket to wear. I knew I wasn't in Africa anymore.

When I got inside the terminal I was totally confused; I had no idea where to go. Large numbers of people rushed in every direction. I wondered where all these people were going in such a hurry. A strange woman walked up to me and said, "Welcome to Frankfurt, Germany, Mr. Eric Wowoh." I did not know this woman; I had never seen her in my entire life. I asked her how she knew my name, and she said, "You are one of my clients, and I identified you from the bag you are carrying. My job is to receive refugees like you and help you in the transit process to your final destination." She added, "I work for the International Organization for Migration, and I am here to help you with food and flight connections."

Shortly after that, we all boarded another Lufthansa flight to Chicago's O'Hare International Airport. When we arrived in Chicago we got off the plane, and again people were moving everywhere. We saw immigration lines for U.S. Citizens, Permanent Residents and Visitors. We did not know which line to take because we did not know what we were.

After a little while, an immigration officer met us in the terminal and welcomed us to the United States of America. He asked us to hand over our bags and told us the American people had given us this opportunity to come to the United States. He said we could stay in the U.S. forever in peace and never had to go back to Africa if we didn't want to. Our bags were taken into a little room, and we were told to wait outside for several hours. Then our fingerprints were taken. That was a very frightening experience. To this day, I still don't know exactly what was in my IOM bag I carried across the world for nearly twenty-four hours.

From the airport in Chicago we were taken to our flights to the various cities where we would be living in America. I was told I would first take a plane to Houston, and from there I would catch another flight to Lafayette, Louisiana.

When I got off the plane in Houston, I was in the middle of a massive international airport. I was once again totally confused. I did not know anything about finding boarding gates, catching the train in the airport terminal or reading flight schedules on computer screens. I walked in circles for hours, not knowing where to go. I missed several flights to my destination in Louisiana until I finally asked a shoeshine man if he could help me. He did, and I finally was able to board the last plane for the day to Lafayette.

15

Life In Lafayette, Louisiana, U.s.a.

I arrived in America on August 28, 2006, with no luggage, no passport, no identification, no phone, no money, no e-mail address or Twitter or Facebook account, no home address and no friends or acquaintances. I didn't even know how to use an ATM machine. My entire world had changed in just twenty-four hours. Although I didn't understand it at the time, I was sent to Lafayette as part of a refugee resettlement program sponsored by the United States Conference of Catholic Bishops Migration and Refugee Services.

The Lafayette airport was quite small in comparison to the Houston and Chicago airports. Immediately after I stepped off the plane, a strange woman introduced herself as Ms. Margaret, my caseworker. She said she would be helping me for the next six months. The title "caseworker" was a negative term to me. After my time in jails in Africa, I thought it meant I had committed a crime and a case was against me in America. This was the first of many culture-shock experiences.

As Margaret drove me from the airport through Lafayette, down Evangeline Throughway to Johnston Street to my new apartment, I didn't see any people walking in the streets. It was like a ghost town. "Where are all the people?" I asked.

She said they were all in the cars driving by. I was shocked to learn that in America everyone had a car and drove to work or school. She also said, "If you don't have a car, it will be hard to get around." That worried and amazed me. In Africa people are always walking around. They seek directions by asking other people in the community.

"So how do you people in America drive around in your cars and still know where you are going without asking people for directions?" I asked.

"We have something called GPS," she said. "It's a little computer device we can use for directions when we travel. You are just arriving here, Eric. You will understand these things with time."

She took me to my first apartment building called the University Place Apartments located near the University of Louisiana at Lafayette campus. I was struck by the bright, bright lights in the apartment and the cleanliness, especially the spotlessly clean carpets on the floor. The air conditioner was on, and I was freezing. My caseworker showed me how to control the temperature. "If it's too hot or too cold," she said, "you can adjust it." This was another huge culture shock for me.

"Where I am from, when it's hot, it's hot, and there's nothing you can do about it!" I said to her.

When I went into the bedroom I was overwhelmed by the king-size bed and all the pillows on it. Who needs that many pillows? I wondered. In my whole life I had never slept in a bed like that.

She showed me a microwave, but I couldn't imagine how it cooked food without wood and fire. A refrigerator was full of food—chicken, butter, cheese, milk—so much food—way too much for one person! My caseworker said she would refill it for me every week! I was already beginning to think about how I could send some of that food back to

Liberia where it was needed. Then she left and said she would check back with me later.

I felt as if I had landed on a foreign planet all alone with no backup plan. I was used to being surrounded by people and gathering together every evening and sharing stories. Now, instead of voices, I heard strange sounds and noises from traffic. That night I slept on the carpet and prayed, "Lord, I know You can hear me. You brought me here. What is my mission and the reason for all of these things that are happening to me and around me?"

One day my caseworker told me I needed to learn how to eat out at a restaurant. "Most Americans eat out," she said. She took me to Outback Steakhouse. I was amazed. They had televisions on the walls, so many utensils to eat with and an incredible number of choices on the menu. I had to make decisions about what to eat and drink. I didn't know how to order. My caseworker ordered a steak for me. When it was brought to the table, I was so overwhelmed I couldn't eat it. The waitress cleared it away. When she returned, I asked if I could take the leftover steak home, but she said it had already been thrown away. I couldn't believe it, so I asked to see where. She took me outside and showed me the dumpster. It was filled with discarded food. I wanted to salvage all that food and send it to Africa to help feed starving children.

From then on, my mission became sending money and food to both the refugee camp and Liberia to help people. I talked to my caseworker about sending money back to Liberia, and she sent me to talk with my refugee program coordinator at the diocese. He was a Vietnamese immigrant who had been in the United States for about forty years. "What you are trying to do is important," he said, "but there are five reasons it won't work: The first is that you have been through a traumatic experience, and it will take you five years to heal. You need five years before you can even think about helping others. The second reason is that the people you need to help you accomplish your mission and vision are predominantly white. They have the money and education, but right now they won't listen to you because of the history of corruption and war in Liberia. The third reason is you don't have a good enough education, and a ton of paperwork is involved with founding an international nonprofit organization and forming a 501(c) 3 organization. You need a degree in international development or business or social services, or you need to have experience volunteering in the United States for a nonprofit organization, such as the Red Cross or Salvation Army. The fourth reason is you don't know anyone in America. You have no money, and you can't do this by yourself. The fifth reason is the diocese cannot help you fund this. The money in the diocese can only be used for people like you who are under our care. It is going to take at least five years before you are able to send money back home in Liberia. You need to work hard for those five years, get a home, develop a credit and work history and then think about helping other people in Africa. You can't give to people what you don't have."

As he was talking, I was thinking to myself, "I'm not traumatized. That's nothing but a label, and that's not a good enough reason for not shipping food to Liberia." After he finished talking, I could see no reason why I was in America. I felt I needed to go back to Liberia right then and there. "I can't stay here," I said.

His response was, "The U.S. government brought you here, and you have no passport. You are not a U.S. citizen so you can't apply for one; you can't travel for five years until you become eligible to apply for American citizenship in order to obtain a U.S. passport." He gave me a refugee packet with information on adult education and English classes to help me get acclimated. "We can't do anything for you until you begin the refugee resettlement process we have laid out," he said.

Resettlement was a foreign concept to me. I had been wandering for so many years that I had no idea what it meant to resettle. I had made a promise to the people of Liberia, and I could not forget them.

After that conversation I became aggressive and vocal about wanting to go back to Liberia to help people. When the government gave me money I began wiring it to the people in the refugee camp and Liberia. When my caseworker came for an evaluation, she discovered I was sending the money I was supposed to be using in America back to Liberia. I was belligerent and refused to cooperate or fill out any forms or sign them. She left. The diocese changed my caseworker to a man from Cuba.

I started a two-week fast and prayer regimen. I was not going to compromise. I had a special burden for the refugees I had left in the camp and the helpless Liberian children who were victims of circumstances beyond their control. The war in Liberia had killed more than 250,000 people. It had destroyed the whole country, wiped out an entire generation and taken countless lives. I was a victim of that violence, and I didn't want any other child to go through war and experience what I went through as a child, not on my watch. I became very defiant.

I arrived in America with a very heavy burden on my heart to do what I could to reduce the suffering of the people of Liberia. Day after day the weight of my own personal story, the weight of the stories of those I left behind and the weight of Liberia's problems got heavier and heavier upon my shoulders. I couldn't sleep. I could not see any purpose to my life in the United States. I may have been physically removed from those terrible situations in the refugee camp and Liberia, but my mind and spirit were still there.

Eric Wowoh and his American partners, Marti Thomas and Heather L. Whitney, visit his parents and family for the first time in 2010. Eric's mother, Kebbeh, is in the middle.

Eric Wowoh (left) and Mr. Desmond Ovbiagele visiting together in Lagos, Nigeria, 2011.

Eric Wowoh staring at his first computer in the Oru Refugee Camp in Ogun State, Nigeria, 2003.

Our first 842 Computer Training Center during and after construction in the Oru-Ijebu Refugee Camp in Nigeria, 2003.

Our second 842 Computer Training Center during and after construction in the Oru-Ijebu Refugee Camp in Nigeria, 2003.

First graduating class of the 842 Computer Training Center in the Oru Refugee Camp, Nigeria, 2004.

Eric Wowoh (left) and Martin Webb working together
in Liberia in 2011.

Group photograph of students, teachers, administrators and our American
partners at the Heart of Grace School in City-View Community Lower
Johnsonville, Montserrado County, Liberia in 2011.

Top view of Heart of Grace School built in Liberia in 2010, our first school
with classes for nursery through grade 12.

A group photo of some of the elementary students of the Heart of Grace School
in Montserrado County, Liberia.

Eric Wowoh and some of his students at Triple "A" School, with classes from nursery to grade 12.

Top view of the Triple "A" School built in 2012 in Gbarnga, Bong County, Central Liberia. This is CAN's third high school campus in Liberia.

In 2006, Eric Wowoh received the RARE GEMS AWARD in Lagos, Nigeria from the Women's Optimum Development Foundation for his contributions to humanity and service to women and children in the Oru-Ijebu Refugee Camp in Nigeria. Award presented by the late Ambassador Segun Olusola.

November 19, 2015, Eric Wowoh was honored with an award from the Migration & Refugee Services (MRS) of the Conference of Catholic Bishops of America. The award was presented to him by His Eminence Donald Cardinal Wuerl Archbishop of Washington DC.

Danny Landry and Eric Wowoh in Lafayette, Louisiana, 2009

Dr. Maureen Brennan and Eric Wowoh in
Lafayette, Louisiana, 2014.

Attorney Edward C. Abell Jr. and Eric Wowoh in
Lafayette, Louisiana, 2014.

Eric Wowoh and a group of children from his hometown, Fissibu, Zorzor
District, Lofa County, Northern Liberia.

A group of teachers and administrators at the Heart of Grace School in Lower Johnsonville, Montserrado County, Liberia.

Eric Wowoh and James Lamar in Lafayette, Louisiana, 2016.

From left, Heather L. Whitney, Fran Clarke, Eric Wowoh and Marti
Thomas visiting with the women in Zuwulo Town,
Lofa County, Liberia, 2012.

Mark and Marti Thomas and Eric Wowoh visiting in
Lafayette, Louisiana, 2014.

Eric Wowoh and Dr. Maureen Brennan and George Thomas (right) in Liberia, 2014.

Dr. Maureen Brennan came to Liberia for the first time to celebrate when her Liberian son George Thomas graduated from University.

Eric Wowh and Jerry Hebert in Lafayette,
Louisiana, 2014.

Breaking the cycle of poverty through education in Liberia.

Together we CAN and we WILL transform Liberia through education.

Change Agent Network is currently educating over 2,000 children in Liberia.

16

Treasure For Liberia

One day I was looking out my apartment window. A dumpster was outside, and piled near it were three computers, a television and an old couch. The irony was it took us years to get one computer in the refugee camp, and now I was looking at three stacked up by the dumpster. I watched all day, waiting for someone to pick up these items. Late that afternoon I went to the manager's office and asked about the computers. "That's all trash," the manager said. "You can take all you want." I gave her my name and apartment number and told her to tell people I would take anything they were throwing away. I tested the three computers I had taken, and they all worked fine. By the end of the week my kitchen was filled with stuff.

In America I didn't have a church, and nobody had invited me to one. In the refugee camp I had gone to church very regularly. I asked around about churches and found out about Lafayette First Assembly. I visited the church and then decided to seek the church's help in organizing shipments to Liberia. I talked with the pastor of the church, and he said he would talk to the board of the church and see what they thought. The board said they couldn't take on this project at that time. One man on the board was from Ivory Coast. He asked me to work with him in the Interfaith Prison Ministry. I joined his ministry and visited prisons to tell my story to inmates. I made some friends.

A month later my rent was due, and I had no money to pay it. I called my friend at the church and asked for funds. The assistant pastor paid half of my rent for one month, but I knew I was on my own after that.

On Thanksgiving Day in November 2006 I was walking down the street by my apartment taking my clothes to the laundromat. I had no idea it was a holiday; I didn't know anything about Thanksgiving. A local news channel van saw me and stopped. Diana Raphael, a reporter, asked me what I was doing on Thanksgiving. I said I was washing clothes. I asked her what Thanksgiving was. She was very surprised I had not heard of Thanksgiving. She asked me where I was from, and I said Africa. She became interested and started asking me more questions. She asked to see my apartment, so I took her there and showed her all the things I had collected from the trash. Yesterday's trash was tomorrow's hope for the Liberian people. She was intrigued and planned to air a story about me on an evening news program on KATC, Channel 3.

She said she would need a contact number so people could get in touch with me, but I didn't have a phone. I went to the mall to buy a wireless phone, but I found out I couldn't get one because I didn't have a social security number. To the phone companies I didn't even exist because there were no public records on me. Nothing with my name showed on the computer. I returned to my apartment feeling rejected, angry and frustrated. I went to my next-door neighbor and asked to use her phone. She gave me her number, and I gave it to the TV station. I didn't tell her I had done that because I wasn't expecting any calls. But after the story aired that evening, calls came in throughout the night from people wanting to help.

My neighbor did a good job writing down the names and phone numbers of all my callers. She came over to my apartment door very, very early the next morning and banged on my door. She was really upset with me. She asked me not to use her number again because she wasn't sure who I was. I told her I had just arrived from Africa and didn't know anybody here, but she wasn't buying it. She said if you just got here, how did you know all of these people who called my phone throughout the night? I knew I had to get money to buy my own phone.

17

Influences In My Life

In 2007 I learned the lesson of a lifetime from Martin Webb, my British friend and brother. He called me from England to say he wanted to come to America to pick me up, so we could visit Liberia together to continue filming his documentary of my life. I was going through a particularly hard time and facing many personal and financial problems, and I was on the verge of giving up everything. I had no money for a trip to Liberia. When Martin called, I told him I was tired and couldn't do this anymore. For a few minutes he was quiet, and then he asked me, "So what do you want to do with your life now?"

"I want to live a normal life," I replied wearily.

"A normal life?" he asked. "Do you think you're the only black man I have ever met from Africa? Why do you think I have followed you around the world for years now, using my own money for flights, taking time off from work and leaving my family? If you were normal, I wouldn't be doing any of this. If you want to live a normal life, good luck. Do not pray to be normal. Right now we need more people like you who aren't normal. Your life is not normal. If you stop now, the work in Liberia stops. All of these people have been supporting you because your life is not normal. Normal people don't make the headline news, and their stories don't make it in books for the generation following to read. I know your life is not normal; that is why I continue to follow you and believe in you. Accept who you are and carry on."

All I could say was, "Thanks, friend." It was a lesson well learned.

I knew I needed a job. I took a walk down Johnston Street in Lafayette through a major business section and stopped at a place called Motor City. The owner gave me a job detailing cars. I didn't know how to drive and had never owned a car. I had arrived in America in August, and by November I was totally on my own. My first focus at Motor City was to determine how to use the company phone to call people who left messages on my friend's phone and wanted to help me. I returned the calls, and soon I was getting more calls at work than the business was.

Out of curiosity I was also learning how to drive. One day I tried driving and scraped the bumper of a car. The business was beginning to get fed up with me, and my computer collecting was taking up more and more of my time. One day a family from Eunice called and said they had two trailers full of computers they wanted to donate. The computers were from a computer company they had once owned. They asked me for the address to my warehouse so they could deliver them. All I had was an apartment, so I gave them the Motor City Car Dealership address that had ample parking space. I met them there, and we took one load to my apartment. When we returned with the second load, the manager of the apartment complex came out and told me I had to shut down the operation; this was not a storage facility. I was given only two weeks in my apartment to move everything out to somewhere else. I was very broken, so I walked to Girard Park in Lafayette and prayed for help.

A week later I went to First Assembly Church and met Jerry Hebert, who owned Premier Cleaners, a dry cleaning company. I needed help, and I asked him if he could help me. He had just lost two workers, so I went to work for him in his location on Johnston Street. I walked there from my apartment. I was seriously late three times because I was working on the computer collection. I got fired three times and got rehired three times as well because Jerry and his family were very nice to me and they wanted to support my work and mission. The weather was cold and rainy one day, so Jerry offered to drive me home. He saw all the computers in my apartment and asked me about them. He wanted to know what I was doing in addition to working for him at the cleaners.

After he left, his wife, Katie, called. "We want to help," she said. Behind their home was a small house that had been built for Hurricane Katrina evacuees who were no longer there. She told me I could live there for free. I told her I would think about it.

I mentioned the offer to some friends from Africa who told me not to trust Katie and Jerry. "We have been here long before you," they said, "and no white family has ever given us an offer like this. This kind of gesture is unheard of. They don't really know you, and they are going to allow you to move into their home to live with them!"

Katie Hebert called me again, and I decided to try it out. Jerry came with a truck to help me move. I moved in and stayed there for three years. I paid no rent, meals were provided, and I could use a warehouse to store the computers and other humanitarian and educational goods free of charge.

18

A Vision: Changing The World

At first, I was totally confused about where, when and how to continue with my humanitarian work in a foreign country that is highly sophisticated, technologically advanced and civilized to the extent that everybody minds their own business. After being in America for a few months I became more optimistic about the future and the success of my own life and work. I got my motivation from just observing. In America all living creatures—even pets—have hope! I got really invigorated when I realized TV carried more than twenty food channels, and some buffets all over the country never ran out of food. The birds of the air were being fed each year. American pets had their own hospitals, a frozen food section in supermarkets, adoption programs, special bakeries, daycare centers, graveyards and even a government protection agency to keep them safe from cruelty! You can appreciate the fact this was quite a shocking experience for me after arriving from a refugee camp where we spent years with little or no food to eat. In the entire human history of our world I believe no nation has ever been as rich and prosperous as that of the American people.

One day a man called to donate computers and asked for my tax ID number. I didn't have one. He said I needed to talk with a lawyer and register my organization as a 501(c)3 to make it legal for tax-free donations. I had no idea how to do any of this. He said I needed to talk to Uncle Sam; I had no idea what he was talking about. Nevertheless, I decided to talk to a lawyer, so I looked in the yellow pages book in my apartment. I was looking for commercial lawyers in the city, and I came across Onebane Law Firm located in River Ranch, one of the more affluent parts of Lafayette.

Edward C. Abell Jr., a lawyer with Onebane Law Firm, said I could come to see him. "You have five minutes to tell me what you want to do," he said, "and then it's $350 an hour."

"I want to change the world," I said.

I wanted to set up a nonprofit. At this point, I had no real job, no proper identification, not even a bicycle to my name; but I wanted to hire the services of a lawyer like Mr. Edward C. Abell Jr., who had a respected law firm in the city. Two weeks later he called me back and asked me to bring two or three board members and a business address. I didn't have any board members. I went on the University of Louisiana at Lafayette campus and met with some African students, Richard Bargblor from Liberia and Chinedu Maduagu from Nigeria. I asked them to be my board members. Richard, a man I knew from the Buduburam Refugee Camp in Ghana, was on the board, and I asked Jerry Hebert, my employer, to be my registry agent. They went with me to Ed Abell's office, and we all signed the paperwork to make Change Agent Network a legitimate nonprofit. Ed said he would send an invoice in the mail. The rest of my board members were very afraid because they didn't know how much this big-time lawyer was going to charge us. I told them not to worry; everything was going to be just fine; I had seen many things much scarier than talking to a lawyer in the one of the most expensive and richest parts of town.

Later I was asked to talk about Change Agent Network to the Rotary Club in the Oil Center in Lafayette. Ed was in the audience. He stood up after my talk and told the crowd that my story had impacted his life. He said in his more than thirty years of law practice I was the first client to come to him saying I wanted him to help me change the world, even though I had no passport, no ID, no job, no bicycle or car and no money. Afterward I asked him about the invoice, and he said he would never send one.

Ed sent me to an accounting firm that helped me get tax-exempt status. The Premier Cleaners where I worked for Jerry Hebert became my first business office in America. Jerry gave me a chair, a desk and a rolodex. In 2008 we were ready to ship the first container to Liberia. I had saved some money from my job, and others contributed to make this happen. We paid ten thousand dollars for a container. The Internal Revenue Service said for any substantial shipment like this to go to Liberia either I or a board member would have to go along with it because of the corruption and lack of infra-structure in post-war Liberia. I needed a passport, but I was not a U.S. cit-izen. When I said I wanted to return to Liberia, people told me it looked as if I didn't appreciate the efforts made to bring me to the U.S. They told me I was being ungrateful to the American people who had given me the opportunity to come to this country.

I called the toll-free number for the U.S. immigration services to see what could be done to help me go to Africa and still be able to come back to the U.S. A man answered and listened to my story. He warned that if I returned to Liberia my life would be in danger. He said the U.S. government couldn't help me and might even deny me re-entry into the country. I told him that if I could take only this one container of computers and supplies it would be worth the risk. He then said, "I think we can help you with a temporary refugee travel document." I paid about four hundred dollars for the document, and it came in the mail just in time.

19

Going Home

I n August 2008 I went to Liberia with the first container. It was the very first time I had been back since I was brought to America two years ago. We began building our first school, Heart of Grace School, in lower Johnsonville in Montserrado County in Liberia. While I was in Liberia I decided to make an effort to find my parents.

I hadn't seen my family since 1990 before I was captured by rebel soldiers. When I was in the refugee camps, volunteers had been unsuccessful in their efforts to find them. Eighteen years earlier I had filled out a Family Tracing Form for the Red Cross but never received a reply about my parents' location. I had no idea where any of my family members were or even if they were still alive.

I returned to my village in Bong Mines, Bong County, and it was like a ghost town. Only a few people were living there, and I didn't know any of them. I learned the Red Cross now had another form that was used for reuniting families. I filled it out and stated the last place I had seen my parents. Three months later the Red Cross told me they had located a family with my same last name in the Guinea Republic, a French-speaking country. I paid people familiar with the camp to take me there and offered a reward.

We arrived at the refugee camp late in the evening. Amazingly, just a few moments later, I saw a woman who looked like my mother walking into the camp after looking for food. My guide approached her and asked if she had a son who had been lost in the war. She said with sadness in her voice, "I don't have a son," and went into her tent. She said that because she thought I had died.

When she came out again, I tried talking with her in our local language, which I remembered. I told her I was her son and that I had survived the war. She was confused because she knew she didn't have relatives in America, and she knew she didn't have a son named Eric. I asked her about my grandfather, my dad's father, and I told her I remembered living with him and going to school. As I talked with her about our family and told her things I remembered, she began to hope I really was her son and started weeping. She tested me with questions, asking how I went to live with my grandfather and how many children were in my grandparents' household. She said back in 1991 people told her I was captured by rebels and turned into a child soldier to fight with the rebels and I had been killed. Slowly she began to believe me.

After that meeting I arranged to move my mother and siblings to Monrovia. No one knew where my father was. Although I was spending all of my money building the school, I managed to send money to my mother to cover their living expenses.

Some of the teachers began questioning where I had obtained the money for the school. People thought I was strange and wondered how I could finance the school. They saw I was doing everything on my own—raising money and paying salaries. "How can he raise money and build schools and still be able to send money to his parents?" they wondered. "We know others who went to America, and they can't do this."

One night my uncle had a dream about a dragon with five heads. It produced money every night and was dangerous. The dragon had the power to control others if they took money from it. He said I was the dragon. My mother believed him and his dream. He warned her about taking money from me. "You don't have any idea how he gets the money or where it is coming from," he told her.

My mother began to think I was using black magic to get my supposed wealth. She thought that if I was really innocent of these charges leveled against me I would have come to the family from the start. As a younger person, I would have shared my vision and mission with them. I would have asked for their help, support and direction. Second, I had left Liberia as a little child who knew nobody. I had never held a real job. So how was I getting all this money? By Liberian standards I was like Bill Gates or Donald Trump. People had no comprehension of how I could get money to build a school. I tried explaining to my mother that people, mostly Christians, back in the States were helping me. I told her God had been at work in my life. When I looked back on my life, it was filled with one miracle after another. All of this was inexplicable to her, as well as to the rest of my family members. They said they knew a lot of Christians, but nobody was doing what I was doing.

My mother became afraid of me, fearing I might do harm to her and the family. She and my uncle wanted to find a way to neutralize the power they thought I had and the powers they believed were controlling me. They called a family meeting in the Red-Light Paynesville Community Market area in Monrovia. The meeting was about persuading me to travel with the entire family to Lofa, our native county, a place they thought had a power great enough to overcome the power in me. They told me that for many years they fasted and prayed to the god of our ancestors to bring me back from the war. "You are back," they said, "but now we have to take you to our native land in Lofa County to appease the gods." I said I didn't want to go, and they threatened to disown me. I wondered how I could convince my family I wasn't a dragon or powered by one.

Later I went to my mother's house. She told me voodoo was in my blood, and it was how I was born. She wanted me to return to our traditional ways and refused to take money from me. I had been sending money to feed my family, but now they wouldn't take it. That night I was sleeping on the floor in my mother's house when my cell phone rang. It was a call from the United States. I changed my accent and tone to talk to the Americans so they would understand me. My mother knew nothing about cell phones, so she freaked out when she heard me. She told my sister to listen to me too. They became even more convinced that my uncle was right. They thought I was talking to myself in a strange voice.

The next day we all went to the last family meeting to decide whether or not I should go back to practicing voodoo. My uncle, chief priest of the family, explained the benefits of living a traditional tribal life. He talked about planting and growing vegetables and then selling them in the market. I remembered doing all these things, and I could see that nothing had changed in the years I had been away. No one in my family had been to school, except me. In my life during and after the war I had been exposed to many things. I said to them, "Show me one person whose life has been transformed by this lifestyle. I don't have a dragon. People called Christians and individuals with good will have helped me." But I couldn't convince them, and I left. Tension remained between my family and me for several years.

20

Reaching Out To The American Public

I returned to Louisiana in 2009, broke and needing to borrow money from Jerry Hebert, my boss. He encouraged me to stop, but I said this was my mission and I could never stop. He told me I needed to find a way to raise money to support the mission. He thought about the diamond resources in Liberia and suggested we talk to a well-known jewelry manufacturing company in Lafayette. I contacted the company, and we were invited to attend a board meeting for their charitable foundation to discuss Change Agent Network and tell my story. At that meeting I met Lou Meinerz.

Lou was active in Trinity Bible Church, which is very mission-oriented. She invited me to visit the church. There I met Marti Thomas, the executive pastor, and Pastor Tim Osborne, the mission pastor, as well as Heather Lecky, a member of the church. Later they all met with me to hear my story. Heather donated two thousand dollars right away for the Heart of Grace School. But the foundation for the jewelry manufacturer wanted more information and asked if anyone from the U.S. had been to Liberia to check out my work and credibility.

Marti and Heather met for lunch and decided to travel to Liberia to see the work. Heather was single, and Marti was married. Marti went home and said to her husband Mark, "I know this is crazy, but God wants me to go to Liberia." I had known them for less than two weeks and had talked with them only a few times. I remember speaking to Mark Thomas at church for less than twenty minutes. They had very, very little information about me.

Marti and Heather told me they were planning a trip, but honestly I didn't believe they would go. Liberia was just emerging from a long and brutal civil war. The Internet was full of horrible reports of kidnappings, rapes and murders. The news reported violence and a lack of security in the country. There was no running water or electricity nationwide. Americans were advised that it was unsafe to travel there. In spite of all these challenges and warnings from the U.S. State Department these two women were determined to go, meet me in Liberia and see firsthand what was going on with the children and adult war survivors. They obtained visas and bought airline tickets.

On the long flight over, both had second thoughts about the venture, but they remembered their initial sense of God's leading and continued to trust Him. "My faith grew so much," Marti said, "as I trusted God on that first trip to such a bruised, broken and scary country. You don't get many big faith-stretching opportunities, but this was one." Their courage and faith are still humbling to me.

The trip was life-changing for both women. Even though they had traveled overseas and participated in other mission trips, they were deeply impacted by what they saw in Liberia and by the people they met. On the day they left Liberia, Heather wrote in her journal: "I am in love with this place. The desperation is everywhere, but the people are warm, friendly, intelligent and hard-working. Everyone wants an education for their children and themselves, followed by job opportunities. It's heart-breaking and heart-warming at the same time. I hope to return to Liberia soon. We will see what God has planned."

Marti returned with a sense that God had changed the trajectory of her life. She had been involved in mission and humanitarian endeavors in Haiti, Guatemala, the Arab world and the Far East, but she sensed that Liberia was the place where she could make a lasting impact. "At my season of life I am beginning to think about the legacy I will leave. It was humbling, thrilling and terrifying for God to ask me to invest my time, my money and myself in Liberia, but I knew this was the beginning of something big. God has not disappointed me; every tiny step I take becomes part of something big and beautiful that only God can do."

Their trip to Liberia lasted just a week. When they returned to the U.S. they took the entire organization out of my hands and ran with it like crazy, talking about it and significantly supporting it at all levels. They talked to their friends, family members, the church congregation of Trinity Bible Church and others about what they had seen. Interest in our project grew rapidly in Louisiana and around the country. They went with me to meet with the officers of the jewelry manufacturing foundation and attest to my credibility and to the fruits of our labors in Liberia.

I was encouraged by the growing interest in our organization, and I thought the meeting with the foundation went well. I became over-confident and stopped talking with people about the work in Liberia. I became complacent and thought I would get help with everything. But one week before I was scheduled to return with a shipment of computers and other supplies I still had no money. I had made all these arrangements, and people were counting on me; but I couldn't do anything more without money. At that point I was ready to give up.

I fasted and prayed: "God, if You are the one who has asked me to do this, please send answers." This was a Wednesday night. I turned my phone off, but on Friday I turned it back on. Several messages had come from Pastor Douglas Broyles, pastor of the Church of Christ in Welsh, a small town about forty-five minutes from Lafayette. He was pleading with me to come speak with his congregation and share my story on Sunday. I reluctantly agreed.

On the way to the church I had two flat tires, and my brake pads went out. I managed to get everything fixed and drove into Welsh, looking for the church. It was a very small church in a manufactured house, and the members of the congregation were very old. Only about ten people were in the congregation, and many had been driven there from a nursing home in Jennings. I was the guest speaker for the service. I told them my story, but I was angry in my spirit because I needed about twenty thousand dollars to be able to make the trip to Liberia that year and pay for shipping the container of supplies to Africa. There was absolutely no way a congregation that small could come up with that kind of money. They were mostly retired people from the nearby nursing home, and they didn't have jobs or paychecks to fund this project. I wondered what I was doing there when I should have been in Baton Rouge, New Orleans, Houston or Dallas at a mega church if I had any expectation of raising this amount of money from a church.

After the service Pastor Douglas Broyles and his wife Joyce took me to the Dairy Queen restaurant for lunch. His wife said she was a teacher and wanted to donate books for me to take to Liberia. She asked me to drive to their house in Jennings to get them. I climbed into the attic to get the books, loaded them in my car and left. It was the journey of a lifetime.

At 10 p.m. that night my phone rang. The pastor called and said he had good news. The church had met, and they all wanted to help me. They wanted to pay for the container and my flight to Liberia. He said he didn't have an address to send a check to, so he would bring it to me. The total amount of the check was twenty thousand dollars to cover the ten-thousand-dollar expense for sending the container and to sponsor six teachers at the school in Monrovia. All that was coming from eleven elderly church members! I was stunned. The pastor said, "We are giving this to you from our hearts. You have the time to do these things we didn't do when we were younger, and we can't do now. If we die today we can feel we did something good. We want to encourage you to keep going."

I still have a relationship with that church, and they are still sponsoring teachers in Liberia. The church members said they want to use their money for schools, not on church buildings. Talking to the pastor and church changed my perspective on things and made me more determined to reach out to all people.

21

The Turning Point

I n 2010 Heather Lecky, Marti Thomas and Martin Webb visited Liberia again. I hadn't talked with anyone about the tensions between my family and me, but they thought something might be wrong and wanted to see for themselves. They told me they wanted to go see my mother. I made excuses, saying the roads were terrible, you had to wade through water to get to the house, and crabs bit anything living in the water. No matter what I said they were still determined to go the next day. They said they were going, and they wanted me to go with them. My mother didn't have a phone, so I couldn't call to let her know.

We all set out for my mother's house. When we were almost there we had to roll up our pants to wade through water. People in the community were curious about the white strangers approaching and came out to see. My mother heard the commotion and ran out to see us. I introduced everyone and said to my family, "These are a few of the people who have helped me raise money and supplies for the schools." We all went into the one-room house, and Marti talked to my mother. She told my mother she has a precious son and thanked her for giving birth to me. She told my mother they were so proud of what I am doing. Then she gave my mother gifts—a nightgown, some jewelry and a handbag with some money— more money than my mother ever had in her life. After that, we all left.

Later my mother asked my sister to call and ask me to come see her. She was still amazed by the visit from two American white women and one British man. Their gift had made her overnight the richest woman in her community. "How do you do this?" she asked. I told her it was by the grace of God. I didn't know how to explain it any other way. She then started to question me about Christianity and my faith. She wanted to know more, so I called the pastor and asked him to come pray with her.

My mother talked to my sisters about all that had happened and then joined a church near her community. She was in awe over what she had seen in me and what she had experienced through the visit of Heather, Martin and Marti. She kept telling me she didn't understand how I could have such a deep love for the people of Liberia after going through so much during the war.

Heather and Marti returned to America, unaware of the impact of their visit. After visiting my mother, they decided to build a house for her. For me, my mission was not about me or my mother. It was about the next generation. All the money I raised was used to build schools, so no money was left to build a house for my mother.

Heather said they planned to raise money to build a house, repair the road and fix the drainage issues. She raised thirty-five thousand dollars and built a house with a kitchen, dining room, living room and five bed- rooms and then gave the keys to my mother. Every day my mother saw things become more amazing. She named the house Kebbeh's Mansion.

This was a turning point in the tensions between me and my family. My uncle still maintained I had a demonic problem, which could only be solved by moving the demon to another person. I never wanted to shift problems from one person to another. Instead I wanted everyone to think about what had happened and go in a new direction. Most of my extended family decided to follow me, but some didn't. My uncle finally agreed I was going in a new direction and stopped standing in my way.

About this time Martin wanted to go with me to my birth village to get information for his documentary film. It was an eleven-hour drive from Monrovia to Fissibu Town where I was born. We planned to stay in the local guest house there. When we got there I saw young men and women about my age walking around with no shirts or shoes. The people had little or no hope beyond survival. They brought back memories of my childhood and the daily work to grow vegetables and get water. I was born in that town, and nothing but abject poverty was there. I thought about my life and how I had gone from this village to living in the United States and booking international flights. These thoughts brought tears to my eyes.

Martin wanted to see the house I was born in. We asked around, and some of the older people remembered where my parents had lived long ago. We found my mother's older brother's house that was across from their house. The house had no windows, no doors and a dirt floor. I couldn't believe I was born in those conditions. I thought the only thing I could do to help was to bring education to the people of Fissibu Town, especially the young people whose futures have been stolen.

We met with the local chiefs, and most of them remembered my parents. They said I was the first person ever to return to the village after the war and years of suffering to offer help. They were amazed I was there in the town eating, drinking and sleeping in the same place they slept. They were very glad I identified with them in their suffering, and that Martin, my white friend and brother, had come with me to visit them. They asked what they could do for me. I said I wanted to build schools for the children's future. The chiefs said they didn't have any money, but they would give us eleven acres of land. I decided that would be the site of Change Agent Network University (CAN-U) and the Change Agent Network High School (CAN High School). These schools would be built in the second largest county in Liberia with the help of local tribes. We would be the first Liberians to make education available, accessible, afford-able and attainable to the struggling people in this area of the country regardless of their economic and social status in society.

22

Expanding The Vision

One year later I met Pastor David Booker of Waco, Texas. He called to say one of his church members, who worked on an oil rig off the Gulf of Mexico, told him I was from Liberia and gave him my number. He went on to explain that he and his wife had visited our website and thought we were doing some amazing things for God in Liberia. He and his wife wanted to go to Liberia and asked if I would take them with me. I said I had just returned from Liberia, but I recommended they not go alone. Pastor Booker told me not to worry about going with them to Liberia. He said they would be just fine going by themselves. They didn't need me to be there, but they wanted me to give them the information about our team on the ground in Liberia. That whole conversation on the phone with Pastor Booker was very bizarre and seemed un-American to me because he was not asking for details of the trip, information about the safety of his life or the structure of operations in Liberia.

I wanted to be in Liberia when Pastor Booker and his wife Kim arrived there and to spend some time with them on the ground, but my nonprofit board said no money was available for me to go back to Liberia at that time. I borrowed some money from a friend of mine and went back to Liberia ahead of them. I had never met the Bookers. I had to go to their church website to see their pictures so I could recognize them among the crowd of people at the airport in Liberia. They spent a week hanging out with us doing ministry work.

Upon our return to the U.S. Pastor Booker invited me to come and speak to his congregation about Liberia and tell my personal story. We didn't have enough money in our account for me to fly to Waco, so I would need to drive my car to Waco to speak to his church. In our nonprofit bank account we were very low on cash. I had just returned from Liberia, and we needed to raise about twenty thousand dollars within a month to meet payroll in Liberia. In spite of all the financial challenges facing the organization I decided to make the trip to Waco, Texas. God has always worked in my life in ways beyond my human understanding.

I spoke to the congregation and shared my personal story and mission with them. Pastor Booker urged his people to surprise and overwhelm me with their love and support for God's kingdom in Liberia. In response to his plea the offering baskets went around this small inner-city church that ministers to the hungry and homeless people in Waco, and the baskets came back with more than twenty thousand dollars in a love offering for the work in Liberia. This response was amazing. The congregation, many of whom needed help and support for themselves, had never made an offering that large for any visiting speaker.

A Texan named Mark lived in Rockwall just outside Dallas. Mark and his daughter Axie had traveled from Dallas to Liberia to dig water wells with the Lastwell, an organization devoted to bringing clean drinking water and the gospel to that entire region. After one of the wells was dug in Bong County in Central Liberia and the water was flowing, the Lastwell organization invited the local people and children to see the well and dedicate it to the Lord. The pastor of the water well team began talking with the children and asking how many were in school. Nobody raised a hand. He then asked how many wanted to go to school and would do so if they could; all of the children raised their hands.

After seeing these amazing kids and their strong desire for education, Axie pleaded with her father to build a school for the children. "No," Mark said.

Without skipping a beat, his sweet little girl replied, "Dad, if you can build a well, you can build a school." Mark conceded she was right, but he reasoned he knew nothing about building a school for children in Liberia.

Mark, along with the entire team, was powerfully moved by the trip and the mission to Liberia. One of the men returning told Tom, a guy who worked for Mark, he really needed to go to Liberia. But Tom had no interest in traveling to Liberia and did not feel as if God was calling him to work in that nation. He said he'd pray about it, but he quickly shelved the idea and didn't give it another thought.

That weekend Tom had to travel to Waco for his grandmother's funeral. She had been instrumental in Tom's coming to know the Lord. He loved her deeply and did a beautiful tribute to celebrate her life. On Sunday, following her funeral, Tom decided to visit a church he knew in the area. Somehow he arrived too late for the service and was very disappointed. He drove away and noticed a small church with services just starting and decided to go in. He took a seat on one of the back rows.

It was that same morning in church that I spoke passionately about Christ-centered education for the children of Liberia and how we were building schools in the country. After attending the service Tom came up to me, crying. He invited me to Dallas to meet specifically with his boss Mark, who wanted to build a school in Bong County, Liberia.

It was again reckless faith on my part to follow this strange man, but I followed him to Lakepointe Church in Dallas and attended a meeting where a handful of men were talking about Liberia and their mission there with the Lastwell organization. Everyone in the room had just returned from Liberia the previous week. The guys were meeting for the first time since their return from Liberia. One of the men in the room was Mark, Tom's boss.

Cowboy Mark, as I love to call him, felt our meeting was divine, and it was a sign from God. He wanted to know more. I talked about our work in Liberia. Afterward he asked me about the cost of building a school, and I told him a six-classroom building would cost fifty thousand dollars. He wrote me a check for forty thousand dollars, and I sent it to our accountant and business office in Louisiana. Cowboy Mark told me he wanted me to return to Liberia without delay and build a school in Bong County for the children. My meeting with him lasted about two hours. He didn't ask me for a reference or documents about Change Agent Network. He didn't even ask first to visit some of the schools we had already built in Liberia before trusting me with that much money. Mark told me he had a successful life, but he felt his life was insignificant in relation to the needs of the world, especially in Liberia where he saw poverty at the highest level.

"My job is to partner with you and fulfill your vision for Liberia," he said.

I went back to Liberia with the money. And with the help of my dynamic team on the ground and the willingness of the local people to work sacrificially we built the biggest school together for a cost of about three hundred thousand dollars. We named the school the Triple "A" School in honor of Mark's wife Teresa and their daughter as a family legacy in Bong County and Liberia. In the past two years Mark has spent a lot of money on this one village, and the school is educating about a thousand children.

One day when Mark and I were having lunch together back in Texas, I told him what he had done when I showed up in Dallas was totally un-American. I had no references and no documents validating my story; yet he trusted me and handed me a check. He told me he was more afraid of what God would do to him if he didn't help than he was of my stealing or mismanaging his money. To date, Cowboy Mark and his family are my biggest donors ever, and he and his family are fully involved with CAN and other nonprofits in Liberia, including, of course, his own— the Lastwell organization. Mark and his family as well as friends are committed to education through CAN specifically to the children and people of Bong County and the country of Liberia.

Tom talked to me about moving an office to Dallas, a city of twelve million people. He said I would be able to reach more people, so he helped me set up an office in the city. It has been a great honor and humbling experience to watch God move in the hearts of people in radical ways. I will never forget this encounter with Him. It is completely crazy, and He has demonstrated to me that He is fully in charge and can do whatever He pleases with His people. I can't wait to see where He takes this relationship and partnership with Cowboy Mark next.

Through His grace, God bestowed upon me the wisdom, favor and leadership ability to lead this organization. By June 2016 we had successfully built fourteen schools on three campuses, and more campuses were under construction in two other Liberian counties. Change Agent Network was educating more than two thousand students with more than two hundred employees on the payroll nationwide in Liberia. More than fourteen hundred students had graduated. Many of them have become meaningful contributors to their society. I am excited about everything in the future because I know who holds that future.

23

Day Of Days In Liberia

I n 2012 Martin and I traveled to Liberia together to film building a school as part of his documentary of my life. One evening we drove home after working late. Six of us were in the car, and Joseph Barker, a Liberian living in Atlanta, Georgia, was driving. It was dark, with no streetlights, and visibility was poor. Pedestrians were walking on the side of the road, many of them wearing dark clothes.

Suddenly, from out of nowhere, an inebriated man stumbled across the road and fell directly in front of our car. We had no time to stop. The car hit him, and the impact threw him across the street. Although the accident was not our fault, angry people surrounded our car. Joe was frightened, and he jumped out of the car and disappeared. I could hear people in the crowd muttering about someone from America killing a Liberian in his own country and on his own streets. I knew things were going to get ugly quickly, and I became concerned about our safety, especially for Martin who is white and from London.

Police quickly arrived from a station about a half mile away. They wanted to take the unconscious man to the station for a statement before proceeding to the hospital, but Martin and I protested, saying he needed to be taken to the hospital first. The police said they didn't have any way to transport him because of his injuries, so Martin and I lowered the seats in our SUV and put the man in the back. An officer said he needed to go with us and got in the car. Suddenly a woman jumped in the car and said the man was her husband. We drove to the nearest hospital and stopped in front of a security guard, who was sitting down. The headlights shone in his face, but still he remained seated and seemed offended by our headlights. He then told me to explain the nature of the emergency.

After I hurriedly tried to explain to him, he said, "Go back to your car and turn off those lights and then come back and talk to me again about what happened." Exasperated at the guard's seeming lack of urgency, Martin nevertheless turned off the lights.

"Now tell me what happened, so I can tell the doctor," he said. "I need to know where and how this occurred, what time and what happened."

"We are wasting time," I said. "This man needs a doctor—now." Finally the guard got up and went inside. A short time later the doctor came out with a beer bottle in his hand and asked us what had happened. Once again I explained. The doctor looked at the helpless man lying in the back of our SUV and hit him on the side of the head.

"What's your name?" the doctor demanded. The unconscious man gave no response. Then the doctor told us the man was not injured, only heavily intoxicated.

"When he sobers up he'll be normal again," he said. "You did well to pick him up. Most would just leave him in the street to die," he said to me, speaking in local Liberian broken English. "You can drop him off outside here, leave him by himself and go about your business. He will be fine when the excess alcohol in his system diminishes."

I found it very difficult to tell my friend Martin what the doctor had said. Rather than attempt to explain such a ridiculous diagnosis, I told Martin we would have to go to JFK Hospital. As its name suggests, the hospital was built by U.S. President John F. Kennedy after he visited Liberian President William Tubman. Although the hospital sustained heavy damage during the civil war, it had since been partially renovated and was the largest and best hospital in the country. By this time it was about 10 p.m., and we had not eaten or rested all day.

Upon arriving at JFK, we walked into the emergency room and saw a group of nurses playing a game at a table. I told them about the accident and said we had a man outside who needed urgent medical attention. They asked the same questions, and I repeated the same story I had told at the other hospital. I was becoming frustrated at everyone's seeming lack of concern for his life-threatening injuries, so I said, "Look—someone is dying. This could be your father, your uncle or someone you know."

One nurse finally told me to bring the man inside. I asked for a stretcher, but she said they didn't have one. I insisted we needed something to carry him on because we thought his back was hurt and possibly broken. She went inside and came outside with a child-sized wheelchair. Knowing we couldn't put him in that chair, we lifted him out of the SUV, tried to support his back without making his injuries worse and carried him into the emergency room.

A doctor on duty asked us to explain our story again. Then he said, "I'll take care of him now. You can go home." The emergency room was filled with patients begging for help. Some were bleeding with horrible wounds; many had been in scooter accidents. We left the man with the doctor, trusting his promise to take care of our accident victim.

By this time it was close to midnight. The police officer and the woman were still in the car waiting for us. The policeman told us we now needed to go to the station to give a statement and turn in the car because it would be needed for evidence if the man died.

We returned to the police station; there was no electricity. The only place to sit was on the prisoner's bench. The lady was still with us. The car was impounded, but no one was around to take our statement. Finally a policeman came over to us carrying a small candle. He said he couldn't take our statement until he had paper, pen and more candles. Then to add insult to injury, he told us we would have to provide the materials. I told the man, "I am a Liberian, but I'm not from here, and I have no idea where to get materials at this time of the night." I also told him Martin was from England and added, "What if you were in England and something like this happened to you?" The policeman said that for fifty dollars he could get the candles and paper.

In ten minutes he had all the materials and began taking our statement. At this point we learned that the lady who had been with us was not the wife of the injured man. The police finally let all of us go about 2 a.m. We were still an hour and a half from where we were staying. I asked the police officers to drive us home since we no longer had a vehicle, but they said they didn't have any extra cars. We told them to use our car to drive us home and then drive it back to the station. They agreed, but we had to pay them one hundred dollars. We didn't get home until 4 a.m.

The next morning around nine we returned to JFK Hospital to check on the man. We were shocked to find him in the same place we left him the previous night, and he was still wearing the same clothes. He had not been touched. I asked for the doctor. Someone said he left because his shift had ended. I talked to a new doctor about the situation. This doctor said there was no way anyone could examine the patient because we had not filled out a patient information form. I told him we didn't know his name, but the doctor said to just use my own name and information. I went to the front reception desk and filled out the forms using my name and contact information. We left again and went to work at the school.

At 4 p.m. we stopped work early so we could check on the man at the hospital. The man had been moved to a bed, but he was still in the same clothes. A nurse told us we would have to provide clean clothes because the hospital did not have clothes for patients. We went home and got some of our clothes and brought them back for him to wear. Next they told us he needed an X-ray.

"Why hasn't this been done?" I asked. "He's been in the hospital now for over twenty-four hours." The nurse said X-rays cost ten dollars, and we could get them done across the street. We paid the money, took the man for X-rays and brought back the results.

"If we hadn't come back to this hospital to see him, what would have happened?" Martin asked. "For lack of ten dollars they would have let him lie there and die."

When we returned the third day we found him talking and asking for food. The hospital had no food to feed the sick and helpless, so the nurse told us we could buy food at a restaurant in Monrovia. We went to a restaurant and bought good food: fried chicken, vegetables and something to drink. We brought the food back to the hospital, and a nurse said she would give it to the man.

That evening we went back to the hospital to check on things. The man was angry because he was still hungry. He had expected us to bring him food. We asked the nurse about the food. She said the patient was too sick to eat the heavy food we had brought, so the hospital staff ate it. The man heard her explanation and thanked us for trying to help. Then he said, "If you leave me here one more day, I'll die. Take me out. I'll go to the police station and tell them I was drunk and the accident was my fault."

His back was sore, so we got him some crutches and went to the police station. After he gave a statement we got our car back. The man asked if we were from Liberia. We told him where we were from, including the fact that Joseph Barker was from Atlanta. The man said some of his family lived in Atlanta. Joe asked about his family and found out they had gone to school together. They both went to the man's mother's house for a big reunion.

That night Liberia became real to me again as I was reminded of the enormous challenges we must overcome if we want to change the story for the next generation. I rededicated my commitment to the people of Liberia to do whatever it takes to make a lasting difference. I believe the problems can be solved. They don't require rocket-science to fix. What makes it personal is that these things have affected me and are happening on my watch. I have a moral responsibility to do something to help. I have seen people who were numb and desensitized to pain and suffering. From the people in the street to the police to the medical personnel, we saw no urgency or concern in responding to pain and suffering.

It's never about us: the politician, pastor, businessperson, doctor, teacher, artist or musician. All of us have to work together to hand over something to the next generation. When we know it's not about us we begin to realize we have a duty to give back. When we recognize it's not about us and decide to work toward a better future for children we experience the true joy and purpose of life. For this reason I am committed to Liberia, the country in which I lost everything and became a victim of a war I did not start—a country that did not care about the future of her children. Liberia is the place where I lost my childhood happiness and joy. We are the lost and forgotten generation of Liberia, but at the same time I view us as the transformational generation of the world.

Part Two

Lessons From Liberia

24

Right People, Right Place, Right Time

For I know the plans I have for you," declares the Lord, "plans to prosper you and not to harm you, plans to give you hope and a future." Jeremiah 29:11 (NIV)

When I sat around campfires at night in refugee camps, I heard talk of America and friends and relatives who had gone to America. I heard about cities like New York and Los Angeles. I had never heard of the state of Louisiana and the city of Lafayette. But in 2006, when I was selected to go to the United States, that's where I was sent. I had serious doubts about going to America, and I had serious doubts about going to a city and state I had never heard of. How would I ever follow through on my promise to help Liberia? Although I didn't know it at the time, it was the right place for me. The challenges I faced in my resettlement helped me acclimate to a new country and helped me put my life into perspective. God led me to Lafayette. It was the right place to launch Change Agent

Network, and in the process, I met the right people to help with this effort. I consider Lafayette my home in America. No matter how far I travel or how long I stay away, I consider this my hometown.

So many people were friendly, kind and hospitable, and I am forever grateful for their help and encouragement along the way. I mention some of the people here to illustrate the heart and soul of those who stepped out in faith to help me. There is not room to mention everyone, so again, I say thank you to all who helped me in any way. You are greatly appreciated.

My first American family support: James and his wife Aimee and family were the very first American family who heard my story and were moved with compassion to assist me in getting acclimated to my new environment. In 2006, after I had just been in the U.S. a few months, I was working at a car wash in Lafayette. It was winter, and I was cold. I was wearing a lightweight windbreaker and flip flop sandals. James and his family saw me and felt sorry for me. They offered to take me to Walmart where they purchased my very first set of new clothes and footwear since my arrival in the country. At that point, I didn't have any money of my own to buy myself anything. Walmart was, of course, another huge culture shock for me. It was ridiculously big and confusing.

I told the family my story. I explained that I did not have any identification to carry out public or international transactions, nor did I know how to send support money through MoneyGram or Western Union back to struggling people and children, my friends, partners and family in Africa. James helped me overcome these challenges. Since then, he and his family have supported Change Agent Network monetarily on a regular basis. He has also used his influence in the community to raise monthly financial support for the people and children in Liberia through Change Agent Network. James and his family are great friends of mine, and they are great friends to Liberia. To this date, we are still working together. I am very grateful, and I thank God for James and his beautiful family and for so many like them!

Danny and the shipping center: Danny is a good man with a great heart for people. I first met him back in 2007 in Lafayette at his shipping center. I went to the center to ask for some free, used boxes for shipping supplies to Liberia in my first container shipment. I walked into his store with no money to buy anything but just hoping that he would listen to my story and cause and try to help me out. Danny is a very good listener. When he saw me, he welcomed me warmly into his store and listened keenly to my story and what I was trying to accomplish. I asked him to kindly donate some of his used boxes so that we could ship our supplies to Liberia. I wasn't quite sure about how much assistance Danny was going to give me, but to my astonishment, he supplied me with all of the empty boxes and packing materials that I needed to make my first shipment to Liberia a resounding success. Danny also donated money to the education of children in Liberia through Change Agent Network, and he served on Change Agent Network's governing board for a few years. For the last ten years, Danny's shipping center has supplied all of our printing, publishing, mailing and shipping containers at a very reasonable cost.

Dr. Maureen and the Rotary Club: Dr. Maureen and I connected in 2009 through two mutual friends of ours. She is a Clinical Psychologist in Lafayette. I was looking for a grant writer, and I spoke with my friend Danny to see if he knew of anyone in the community that could help me out. Danny told me about a woman named Cheryl at an entertainment center located in downtown Lafayette. Cheryl was very warm, nice and welcoming. We spent about two hours talking about my story and what I was trying to do. She then introduced me to Dr. Maureen.

I spent another two hours sharing my story and mission with Dr. Maureen in her office. She is a very good listener. She told me about the

Rotary Club and other opportunities we could explore in the community in seeking funding and other resources for the children and people of Liberia through Change Agent Network. This was my very first time to hear about the Rotary Club and the things they do.

Dr. Maureen donated computers and accessories from her office that day to be shipped to Liberia in the container I was putting together that year. She set up my first speaking engagement at the Rotary Club. She was the first person to introduce me to the corporate American way of running a nonprofit. She also wrote our first grant to her Rotary Club to get funding to pay for blackboards, bookshelves, a water well and student desks at our first academic school, Heart of Grace School in Monrovia, Liberia.

Dr. Maureen personally sponsored my friend, brother and business partner George A. Thomas through university in Liberia. Today, George Thomas is Country Director of Change Agent Network, and he is giving back everything he has received in life to others. Dr. Maureen travelled to Liberia in May, 2014 to meet the Liberian son she had supported through the university. She met his family and participated in George's graduation party. She arrived in Liberia with a huge surprise package for her Liberian son. She presented him with a master's degree scholarship opportunity through the International Rotary Club for him to study abroad. He respectfully refused to pursue his advanced degree program overseas because he wanted to positively impact the lives of many more people with the undergraduate degree he had acquired from the university before he entered a graduate program.

Over the last seven years, Dr. Maureen has introduced us to other Rotary Clubs around the country and encouraged them to get involved with our educational work in Liberia. I am very grateful for the opportunity God has given me to meet and work with a wonderful and caring person like Dr. Maureen.

Yassah's Sisters Livelihood Program: Fran is a licensed Clinical Social Worker and Therapist in Lafayette. When I met her, she questioned me about what I was doing specifically for the women in Liberia. She and others were touched by the story of Yasseh Ford, a single Liberian mother struggling to feed her family. Fran organized a group of women in Lafayette to collaborate with CAN to help meet the needs of women like Yasseh. They formed Yasseh's Sisters, a pay-it-forward program that provides agricultural tools and seeds to single women. The women are given a machete, hoe, ax and bags of peanuts, rice, beans, corn and okra seeds for planting. After the first harvest, participants are to pass along a bag and a half of seeds to another woman. It's a wonderful example of women helping other women. The program continues today with over one hundred participants.

Dennis and Fay: My first speaking engagement and fundraiser for Change Agent Network was held at Freedom Missionary Baptist Church in Eunice, Louisiana. Pastor Dennis and his wife, Fay, heard about my work and invited me to speak. There were fewer than twenty people attending the service, but they raised about $2,000 for education in Liberia. They are still actively helping CAN and have paid for school equipment and filled shoeboxes with school supplies for the children. I'm always grateful to them because they were the first church that believed in my mission and raised money to help.

Ernie and Rose: Ernie and Rose responded to the story aired on KATC when the news reporter saw me walking near my apartment on Thanksgiving Day. Ernie is a veteran who had owned a computer company. When he closed the company, he was left with two truckloads of computers. He was looking for a place to donate them when he heard the story on television about my desire to collect computers for a school in Liberia. They contacted me and then drove the two trucks full of computers to my apartment. They helped me unload the computers and carry them up two flights of stairs to my apartment. Ernie asked me how I was going to ship them to Liberia, and I said I didn't know. He prayed for me in my apartment with the computers. I'll never forget how Ernie and Rose brought me the first large donation of computers and gave me the encouragement to find a way to ship them to Liberia.

25

Rebuilding Liberia

The Bible contains an amazing story of grace, redemption and the rebuilding of a post-war nation that has resonated with me ever since I became a Christian and read this story. It constantly reminds me of my own personal mission and purpose in life as a former refugee and a survivor of violence and torture. It also leaves me with no excuse or reason whatsoever for not bringing real hope and opportunity to a broken, forgotten and lost generation of young people in my home country of Liberia. The story is found in the Old Testament book of Nehemiah.

Nehemiah was cupbearer to Artaxerxes, the powerful king of Persia. In the twentieth year of the reign of Artaxerxes, Nehemiah learned that some of the Jewish people who had survived the Babylonian exile had returned to Jerusalem in Judah. The walls of the city were broken down, and the people were in distress. Nehemiah asked the king for permission to return to Jerusalem and rebuild the city. Artaxerxes sent him to Judah as governor of the province with a mission to rebuild the city. He gave Nehemiah letters declaring his support for the venture and allowing Nehemiah to take timber from the royal forest. Once there, Nehemiah surveyed the damage and enlisted the help of the people to rebuild the walls. Although Judah was surrounded by enemies on all sides—Samaritans, Ammonites, Arabs and Philistines—Nehemiah and the Judeans rebuilt the walls in only fifty-two days, from the Sheep Gate in the North, the Hananel Tower at the North West corner, the Fish Gate in the West, the Furnaces Tower at the Temple Mount's South West corner, the Dung Gate in the South, the East Gate and the gate beneath the Golden Gate in the East.

Whenever I read this story, it gives me real hope, not for money or material things. I am motivated to remain committed to breaking the cycle of generational poverty in Liberia, Africa's oldest democratic nation. Like the prophet Nehemiah who lived in the powerful Persian empire of his time, I see myself living in the number-one country of the world in my days, the United States of America. I see myself as the Nehemiah of my time with a mission to return home to Liberia and rebuild a destroyed and hopeless nation. Nehemiah was the cupbearer to Artaxerxes. He knew everything about the king, including the king's power and influence in the world. He lived with the king, the most powerful man on the face of the earth at that time, and he had access to everything in the palace. But Nehemiah did not just sit idly by in the kingdom eating, drinking and merry-making all the time. He did not forget about his suffering people back home or about the destroyed walls of Jerusalem. He did not suffer from self-pity, nor did he complain, blame or play the victim-mentality game against others.

Because I was brought here to the United States of America as a refugee to be given a second chance to live a decent life, I consider myself a cupbearer serving in the palace of our time. I know who the Americans are because I live with them. I eat, drink and interact with them every day. I know what they are capable of doing. I know their influence and power in the world and the resources they have to transform the entire world if they desire to do so.

I can't afford to be quiet and impartial about fighting poverty in Liberia. I was born into it, I was brought up in it, and I lived it. I am not giving an opinion on a subject I don't understand. This is not a piece of research I put together from the Internet to present to you. This is my life and the lives of millions of people. Poverty is a real problem that is killing millions of real people just like us every single day. Poverty is aggressive and deadly. Therefore, our response to it and our collective efforts to destroy it must be even more aggressive and more deadly than it is.

Liberia is a very small country with about 4.5 million people. It is about the size of the state of Ohio. The problems in this country can be solved in no time. The solution is very much possible; we can see it, we experienced it, we have tried it, and it works.

26

Things That Are Unchangeable

Now, looking back, I believe my life is nothing but a collection of stories containing different events, good and bad, that constitute my journey in this world. God wrote and published both the good and bad long before my arrival, and the manuscript was handed over to me at birth with a charge to be a good steward of its contents by sharing it with others. Therefore, I cannot change the storyline or alter anything in my storybook because I did not write it. The best thing for me to do in order to live a fulfilled life is simply to embrace myself by accepting and loving my story no matter how terrible, shameful or beautiful it might be. My story is my story, and your story is your story.

The solution to all of my pains, struggles and worries lies in the full understanding and implementation of the story of my life. God did not consult with me before creating me to be a Liberian from Fissibu Town in Lofa County, Northern Liberia, where there is no running water, no electricity, no education and, of course, very little opportunity and hope. He did not ask me about my opinion or feelings about being born a black man from Liberia, West Africa. Neither did He ask me how I felt about

Mr. and Mrs. Wowoh becoming my parents. I never chose my DNA, the color of my skin or even my tribe. If God had given me the opportunity to choose and write my own life story and decide my destiny, I would have perhaps chosen a different nation, skin color, parents or tribe and changed virtually everything in my entire life. But for reasons best known to Him He did not seek my opinion concerning these matters. That's why I tell people everywhere I go today that this is not my own story because I did not write it myself. I don't think I would have written such a hard-hitting story of pain, endurance, long-suffering and uncertainty, as well as grace and redemption, about my own life and at the same time be proud to share it with the whole world. Therefore, this is not Eric Wowoh's story but God's. He only used my life as a pen in His hands. I am honored and humbled to be a good and faithful steward of this story.

For me to know and understand where I am going with my life at the end of this journey, I must first be able to comprehend the story of where I have come from, knowing this will definitely help me understand where I am right now. And my current station in life will help determine my final story at the last bus stop!

My life story today has given me a lasting work and purpose by giving me something powerful to share with others and something significant to live for, enabling me to impact my world and reshape the future, as well as create the culture of the next generation. Now I sit and look back at everything that happened to me during those darkest days of my life, and all I can say is, OH, IT IS JUST GOD!

I accept the things I cannot change and have learned to live with those things and stop complaining.

Nobody can share my story better than I can because it is my life, and I am living and walking in it. It is not a research paper, Internet research information or something I read in a book or heard about.

This is the reason I did not change my nationality to become an American citizen, and I will not change anything. The United States of America is a wonderful place to be because it is the most prosperous nation in human history, as well as the most powerful and influential nation on planet Earth. I sincerely believe it would be the worst mistake of my life to change my identity, thereby effectively disowning my own country, people, my family, history and heritage. If God wanted me to be an American, I believe that from the very beginning of time He would have made either my mother or father come from the U.S. Both of my parents were created Liberians, in line with His divine plan and purpose for my life. Therefore, the best thing I can do to live a happy and fulfilled life is to cherish and be proud of who He made me to be. I must appreciate my identity and embrace myself because, in my opinion, this is the path that leads to gratitude, personal acceptance and more favor from God— He makes no mistakes!

We become ungrateful when we forget about our past!

When I lose my personal identity and background I lose everything, because I will never be content with who I am and what I truly have. I will have then become a victim of the comparison trap, trying to be like everybody else around me by living my life in pretense and self-denial, counterfeiting everything, trying to measure up through appearance and performance. This kind of behavior will eventually lead to a lot of other complications in life such as a never-ending restlessness, a lack of personal confidence and dissatisfaction. Living in this manner creates an emptiness in life that nothing can fill. The solution to anger, frustration, bitterness and violence is self-discovery of my God-given identity. Discovering my identity ultimately helps me remain calm by knowing my purpose in life and keeping everything in its proper perspective.

27

Making A Difference

When I first started thinking about providing help to Liberia, I was only thinking of shipping old books and computers. With the help of others I was able to expand the vision and bring educational opportunities to the people.

I want to see change for this generation, and my goal is to fight poverty through education. I want to see my country free of physical, mental, relational and spiritual poverty. It's hard for people to think for themselves when they have no education. They think the way people in power tell them to think. My goal is to enable people to take full responsibility for their own lives and the lives of their children.

When I arrived in the United States in 2006, I was exposed to the secret of American prosperity—education. I saw the enormous possibilities available when you have an educated public. When I learned to use a computer I had something to give back to my community in the refugee camp. I had a skill and a purpose. Being in America showed me what more could be done, and it gave me hope to return to Liberia and be a change agent. I don't want to bring American culture to Liberia or bring Liberian culture to America either. That is why I am not asking for the American Dream. I want to break down the walls and build bridges for all of us to connect and work together in finding solutions to the issues, such as poverty, that affect us all as human beings. I want to bring education to the children and people of Liberia so they can learn to take control of their own lives and destiny.

My goal is to create a formal education system in Liberia by building a holistic center that would include a cafeteria, guest house, cultural center, school, health and worship center in each county. We now have a model in three different counties in Liberia. We CAN and we WILL replicate this proven and tested model in the remaining twelve counties in the country by the end of this decade 2020. It is an example of how individuals with a vision can transform their country. Our program brings educational opportunities to the people where they live and work. Their job is to take over the school and center and manage it for the children. Change Agent Network is the bridge between the givers and the receivers, and we provide training and leadership. Resources come from America and other friendly nations; the land, labor and teachers come from Liberia.

The war brought bitterness and destruction because of decisions the earlier generations made. I want to break the cycle. God has laid this on my heart.

Had it not been for God, I would be bitter; I would be seeking revenge and trying to pay back the people who hurt me. God has given me a heart of forgiveness and repentance, and I feel a moral responsibility to respond to the need in Liberia. I have been given a purpose in life I never imagined possible. In all my brokenness, the more healing I receive, the more I can give to others.

I saw the worst life has to offer. Then God brought me to the United States to see the very best the world has to offer. I've been at the bottom, and I've seen what's at the top. It's not how much you have; it's what you do with what you have that makes a difference.

28

Why Christ-Centered Education For Liberia?

W hen I came to the United States of America in 2006 I couldn't rest or concentrate on anything. The needs and pains of the innocent children and people of Liberia weighed heavy on my heart. While I was a refugee in 2002, around age twenty-three, a friend, Desmond Ovbiagle, gave me a computer. I learned how to use it and began training other refugees from all over Africa. By the special grace of God I have been able to impact the lives of many individuals across the world. Change Agent Network was born as a result of that one single desktop computer that was given to me in the refugee camp. Education from one computer changed my life forever and gave me something significant to give back to society. This is why I strongly believe Christ-centered education is the key to breaking the cycle of poverty in Liberia. I describe it as Christ-centered education because we want first and foremost to give the children a solid foundation in Christ before teaching them how to read and write and earn a good living.

I think our society has spent a lot of time and resources teaching people how to earn a good living and not how to live well. We have taught our children that life is all about them by telling them to go to school and be smart, so that they can graduate with good grades, get a well-paying job, and live life as though there is no tomorrow. We have failed to teach and demonstrate to young people the moral and physical responsibility they have to leave the world better for the generation following. I think the selfless and compassionate personality of Christ is what we need to heal the broken, messed-up society of our time. Christ-centered education is the best gift we can ever give individuals to liberate them from all forms of poverty—physical, mental, relational and spiritual. When a person dies, he or she takes their gift with them into the grave; it is an eternal gift that is not transferable. You can't hand it over to your kids or loved ones. Everything else you leave behind in this world can be stolen or falsely taken away from your children and family, thereby creating serious problems for them. Transformation comes through information. Education is the most powerful tool we have to fight poverty. Slaves back in the days were not allowed to be educated because education would give them the power of knowledge and true freedom to determine their own destiny. Today, in my honest opinion, we are still in the business of slavery because we are not doing enough to educate the poor and the children of today who are the leaders of tomorrow. They are going to end up in intellectual slavery. This new form of slavery has nothing do with buying and selling people or working them on plantations with chains on their necks and legs.

Change Agent Network serves as a bridge between the people of Liberia and those living in the United States and the rest of the world. Giving is good for both the givers and receivers. The givers receive healing for their body and soul by helping someone else in need, and the receivers experience healing for their physical needs. I hope my story helps others deal with problems in whatever world they are living. We have much to do. We have to band together to fight all forms of poverty. We live in a global community that is inter-connected. All of us need to fight poverty in all forms—physically, mentally, relationally and spiritually—in order to help make our worldwide community be a better home for all of mankind. "Educating the mind without educating the heart is not education at all."

29

Breaking The Cycle Of Poverty Through Education

The human spirit yearns to be free and self-sufficient. Waiting for an aid worker to come every few weeks with food and clothing does not meet this need. Although a starving person is certainly glad to receive the necessities of life, having to wait for someone else to provide them leads to resentment, unrest and possible revolution.

Those of us who lived through the horrific events of the last civil war must lead by example. It is now up to those of us who survived the carnage to pick up the pieces and rebuild. We must create a country where all citizens feel they have a part and a responsibility to preserve it for the next generation.

Education empowers people and frees them from physical and mental slavery. Education is the key that opens the door to true freedom, independence and empowerment for every human being. That is the reason why in the days of slavery the slaves were not allowed to be educated.

When we don't fully invest in the development and promotion of education for impoverished people, we enslave them both mentally and physically. We deny them the ultimate power to think independently, creatively and innovatively to unleash their potential. In my opinion and experience, our modern-day slavery is not the physical buying and selling of human beings and transporting them to plantations around the world in chains. Instead, modern-day slavery is that we keep our fellow human beings physically strong, but mentally weak. To remain in authority over the lives of others, dominate and dictate the lives of our children and people, we feed and clothe them, keep giving them stuff, keep them physically strong but give them no education. They have no time and opportunity to think and decide their own future and that of their children.

My message to every leader and parent around the world, Africa and Liberia in particular, is that if we truly want the best for our children's future and the people we care about then we must make education our number-one priority when it comes to investment and legacy building. Once the human survival needs have been met and some stability created, our next step toward freedom and development MUST be education of our people at all levels. Education will definitely bring about economic prosperity for all. Freedom without educational emancipation is useless!

Afterword

Testimony To Liberia

I n early 2010 my life seemed to be completely together. I was a single, forty-two-year-old woman with a fantastic career. I had been blessed with the opportunity to travel the world, and I was in a serious relationship with Chris Whitney, the man I believed God sent to be my husband. So when Chris suddenly and unexpectedly ended our relationship in February that year I was shaken to the core. At this time I had been actively pursuing a relationship with the Lord for a few years and had prayed extensively about our relationship, believing the Lord had indeed identified Chris as "the one." My inability to reconcile what I believed I was being told in prayer with my new reality was overwhelming to a point that I barely left my house except to go to the office and Trinity Bible Church. During this time I wrestled continuously with God for control over this situation; but God clearly told me to leave Chris alone. It was in my complete brokenness that I finally surrendered all I had, including my very life, to the Lord and told Him I would do whatever He wanted of me.

During the summer of 2010 I attended a Bible study centered on a book titled *The Hole in Our Gospel: What Does God Expect of Us?* by

Richard Stearns. When I signed up for the class I had no idea what the subject matter was; all I knew was that Marti Thomas, my spiritual rock, was leading it. For those who have not read the book, it is about world poverty and how the Western church has politely ignored the issue of poverty, choosing the popular prosperity gospel instead. Being a successful American businesswoman, I found the message really hit home. I personally believe education is the key to breaking the cycle of poverty, and as a single woman, my education means everything to me. But what was I supposed to "do" about all the thoughts racing through my head because of the Bible study? This was a question I posed to the Lord continuously. In the moment I met Eric Wowoh and listened to him tell me his life's story and about the schools he was trying to build in Liberia, I "knew" my meeting Eric was no coincidence and that this was what God wanted me to "do."

Eric and I spoke for only thirty minutes that first meeting, most of which I spent completely in awe that this was happening. But later that day I received a call from Lou Meinerz, the woman who introduced us. She told me more of Eric's story, including that her employer was interested in whether anyone from the States had been to Liberia to verify Eric's work before he made a sizeable donation. That was it. I was going! But what was exciting to me was terrifying to my family. My mom, Marci Lecky, and I were frequent travelers; but when she got online to learn about Liberia and saw images of a war-torn country full of child soldiers and abject poverty she panicked! She called my sister, Elizabeth Pham, and they called me crying and begging me not to go. I had never seen either of them behave this way before, or since. Because I could not rationalize away their concerns I finally had to make it clear this was what the Lord was asking me to do, and I was going, no matter what.

I cannot say I did not have at least a few concerns for my safety or for what I would experience, and I was grateful Marti and I were going together. But you will never walk on water if you do not trust God enough to get out of the boat; and I am so glad I took that risk.

I went to Liberia believing my role was to check out Eric's work and lend credibility to his organization back in the States. Instead I realized the Lord was using Marti's and my presence in Liberia to send a message of hope for change to a desperate people. Seriously, this is much heavier than what I signed up for! It is very easy to avoid having to stare poverty in the face in America but not in Liberia. The entire country is poor. Through my interactions with the community I learned what "give us this day our daily bread" actually means. We have pantries full of food; but in Liberia if you don't sell your wares in the market, you and your children don't eat that day. The same goes for tomorrow and the next day. In some cases I was walking and talking with people who had not eaten in a week, without exaggeration. At first the locals, many of whom had never met a white person, were afraid and standoffish. But by the end of our week, fear turned to friendships, and the women started approaching me with notes that asked for help. Much to my amazement, they did not ask for money or for food; they asked me to help them educate their kids.

That first week in Liberia completely changed my life. It was analogous to the concept that "the blind could see." When I returned I had to deal with a rush of emotions ranging from excitement and a heightened gratitude for all the blessings in my life to heartbrokenness for the desperation I had seen. I felt guilty every time I ran the water in my house. I must admit I cried every night for a month and a half, and I struggled to keep from bankrupting myself by responding to every need. But instead of allowing this to break me I used the inequity I had witnessed to serve as motivation to do what I could to support Eric and his work. Through this experience I learned God is not asking us all to be the "Erics" of the world or to solve all of the world's problems. He is simply asking us to do our part based on the gifts and talents with which He has blessed us and in accordance with His will for our lives.

After more than four years apart, the Lord brought Chris back into my life, and we married in November 2015. But Eric Wowoh and my family and friends in Liberia and at Change Agent Network are still a major part of my life. One of the underlying principles upon which CAN was founded and operates is that "we will sacrifice our lives today for the generation tomorrow." I have met plenty of people who do great work with a variety of organizations, but I have never met people who sacrifice on the level Eric and his core team members do. They have chosen to forego the comforts of family and financial stability in order to dedicate themselves to creating opportunities for the people of Liberia so as to rebuild their nation. Being from Liberia, they have no concept of "political correctness" and are unafraid to reference God in every conversation, giving glory where it is appropriately due for all they have. Through their examples, I am much bolder in my faith and have a much deeper appreciation of what it means to live on faith and faith alone. Not only are these men my brothers, they have been my teachers and guides through an unfamiliar world where faith moves what seems to be insurmountable mountains and hope in the Lord overcomes desperation and despair.

———Heather Lecky

Important Dates

1817 American Colonization Society (ACS) formed in U.S.

1820 ACS sends first ships to Africa

1821 ACS acquires Cape Mesurado

1835 Six more colonies established

1838 Colonies come together to form Liberia

1839 Country receives official name of Commonwealth of Liberia

1841 J. J. Roberts becomes first governor

1842 Liberia composed of original colonies and four additional colonies

1926 Firestone creates world's largest rubber plantation

1974 Eric Wowoh born

1982 Samuel Doe leads coup d'etat against President Tolbert; People's Redemption Council established

1989 Liberia Civil War begins

1990 Eric becomes a refugee

1992 Eric becomes a Christian

2002 Eric learns how to use a computer

2003 Eric begins teaching other refugees

2002 842 Computer Training Center opens in Nigeria

2006 Eric goes to America

2007   CAN is incorporated

2008   Eric ships first 40-foot container to Liberia; first academic school built in Liberia

2012   CAN begins building school in Fissibu, Eric's hometown

2015   CAN opens office in Dallas, Texas; Eric receives recognition from Migration and Refugee Services of the Conference of Catholic Bishops of the U.S.

2016   Two containers of educational supplies, medicine, food and household items sent to Liberia

CPSIA information can be obtained
at www.ICGtesting.com
Printed in the USA
LVOW05s0343230617
539109LV00016B/607/P